CULTURE UNVEILED

A COMPENDIUM OF RESEARCH-BASED LITERARY CRITICISMS AND BEYOND

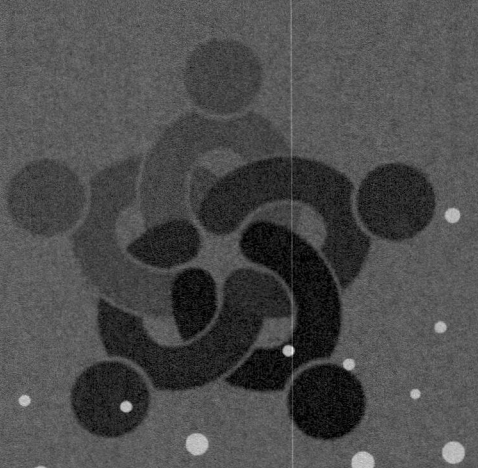

SHERILL ASIS-GILBAS

Culture Unveiled

A Compendium of Research-based Literary Criticisms and Beyond

ISBN 978-1-257-63128-5

Published by Lulu Book Publishing

United States of America

Dedication

To my family, for better understanding of our roots.

To Tatay and Nanay, for the unending stories of our lives.

Cultural identity is as important as one's name.

SAG

Acknowledgments

The author is forever grateful to the support of the Sorsogon State University, her family, friends, and relatives.

To God, be the Glory.

Contents

Preface

This compilation of five research articles served as a Reader for research and literary enthusiasts. The materials are various literary genres from prose and poetry as well as prose narratives. The articles utilized various theories and approaches focused on identifying cultural aspects.

The first article identified culture as an inherent factor in addressing the questions of gender roles in Philippine fiction. It employed Gadamer's Hermeneutics to discuss the binary opposition of marriage and infidelity, faithfulness, and unfaithfulness, along with its implication to the couple and the society in general.

The second article intended to unravel reasons behind the strange affection of the Millennials to the literary works with deformed characters or scary themes. This paper used a descriptive- qualitative type of research anchored on the theories of the grotesque. It was used as an analytical tool to present the motives behind the Millennial's allure to the literary materials with scary or deformed characters.

The third article employed qualitative-descriptive approach of literary criticism, anchored on the theory of New Historicism and formalist contextualist approach. The findings revealed that the poems are good sources of information about the image of the places in terms of physical and cultural milieu.

Moreover, the fourth article focused on the study of legends as prose narratives. The paper attempted to study the classification, structure, and themes of the legends of Sorsogon City and their variants. The results emphasized the difference between the prose narratives from fiction, having its own distinct elements. Through an interpretative type of literary criticism, which was validated using the parameters of Manuel's vertical and horizontal tests.

The last article considered water as both material and non-material culture of the community. It focused on the anthropological approach that deals with water utilization, valuation, and perspectives on water safety of the residents. Thematic analysis was employed from the informants' in-depth interviews. This paper found out that the socio-economic aspect of the community was affected by the availability of water, water use, and how people value water.

It is therefore hoped that through this compilation of articles on culture, more scholars may develop the love of one's culture. Every scientific article originated from a single idea, and every idea has a story to tell when properly treated with appropriate tools of research. All the articles in this book aims to promote understanding after appreciation.

CHAPTER 1

Facets of Machismo and Maternalism in Fictional Philippine Settings

Published in JPAIR Multidisciplinary Research
http://dx.doi.org/10.7719/jpair.v16i1.273

Print ISSN 2012-3981 • Online ISSN 2244-0445

ABSTRACT

The legal implication of infidelity in Philippine law serves as an initial display of "machismo" that reflects the propensity and pervasiveness of its concept in Philippine society. As a response to society's partiality to male's gender role, the gender role of women called "maternalism" has surfaced. This gender role identifies itself as a manifestation of society's concept of gender roles including double-standard machismo. This paper aims to disclose how desire is depicted as justification to the existence of machismo and maternalism in selected Philippine short stories like "Magnificence," "Of Fish, Flies, Dogs and Women," "The Chieftest Mourner," "Thirsty is the Arid Land," and "Wedding Dance." This paper also supports the concept of desire with pleasure principle and tripartite model of Sigmund Freud's psychoanalysis. The paper's critical point focuses on how infidelity is reflected in said stories, thereby leading to understanding its concept as manifested by characters' gender roles. This paper also employs the descriptive literary analysis anchored on Hans-Georg

Gadamer's hermeneutics. In addition, the paper also discusses the binary opposition of marriage and infidelity, faithfulness and unfaithfulness, along with its implication to the couple and the society in general. The paper identifies culture as an inherent factor in addressing the questions of gender roles in Philippine fiction.

***Keywords** - Literature, machismo, maternalism, hermeneutics, psychoanalysis, literary analysis, gender roles, descriptive design, Philippines*

INTRODUCTION

Halo-halo is one of the favorite desserts of Filipinos. Its peculiar taste from different ingredients such as ice and milk topped with creamy leche flan and cheese and at the bottom part, the variety of flavors like sweetened beans, banana, jackfruit, colored gelatin and sugar makes it a popular choice of desserts especially during the summer. Its wonderful taste could be related to Filipino cliché, *habang lumalalim, lalong sumasarap*, which literally means the bottom gets more delicious when one eats from the top without mixing the ingredients at the bottom with those at the top. The cliché is actually a nice metaphor for life: more experiences good or bad means a better person

People love to feel ecstatic, they laugh, feel betrayed, they cry, forgive, and then they learn. As one grows older, he or she acquires a conglomeration of different experiences that come with varying emotions and reactions. There are laughter, betrayal, crying, forgiveness, and learning—and this mixture of situations result in a person accepting what he or she cannot control. Happiness is a choice. Such is the researcher's perception about choice-making in relation to gender roles in Philippine society as reflected in the prose narratives which this paper put under study.

A person's idea about marriage and infidelity is a result of his or her exposure to culture and his or her upbringing and experiences. In the Philippines, which is predominantly Catholic, a man and a woman deciding to be united in matrimony are expected to vow to remain faithful to each other; therefore, when infidelity comes into the picture, that marital vow is broken. According to Gonzales (1991)- quoting Medina in his discussion of *The Filipino Context of Infidelity and Resilience,* extra marital relationships range from casual relationships to the keeping of a querida or paramour. Given that most Filipinos are Catholic, one who strictly adheres to his or her faith actually considers marriage sacred, hence indissoluble.

In Philippine law, the infidelity of the husband differs from that of the wife in terminology and in punishment level:
"Concubinage is committed by any husband who shall keep a mistress in the conjugal dwelling or, shall have sexual intercourse, under scandalous circumstances, with a woman who is not his wife, or shall cohabit with her in any other place. (Article 334 of the Revised Penal Code or RPC). Adultery means the carnal relation between a married woman and a man who is not her husband, the latter knowing her to be married, even if the marriage be subsequently declared void (RPC Article 333)."

Legally then, the Filipino married male who keeps another woman temporarily is committing the crime of infidelity called concubinage. The Philippine Law favors men committing infidelity considering the difference between a conviction for adultery and concubinage. The proof of sexual intercourse is enough in adultery, but in concubinage, the prosecution must prove that sexual intercourse is under a scandalous circumstance or that the husband keeps a mistress and cohabits with her. In addition, the penalty for adultery is the same for both woman and man (prision correctional medium and maximum); in concubinage, however, the penalty for a man is lower by one degree (prision correctional minimum and medium). The concubine is given a separate penalty called *destierro*. It is a penalty based on the proximity or distance to the scene of the crime. Indeed, the law is reflective of society's concept of gender roles, along with the idea of double- standard machismo.

"Men by nature are polygamous,"—one often hears this cliché and passé to justify. This excuse relates to what is known as "machismo" complex which encourages some Filipino men to take on a highly sexual role, egged on and verified by the peer group to which he belongs. True machismo also tends to be measured in terms of the number of affairs a man maintains and the number of children he sires either with his legitimate wife or his mistress or mistresses.

This paper deals with the various types of machismo and maternalism in fictional Philippine settings as seen in selected short stories as materials under study. Lumbera (1997) points out that English writing in the Philippines began during the first decade of the 20th century; however, it was only in the 1950's when it began to attain stature as literature. Accordingly, the short story as a literary form entered Philippine Literature through the agency of the English writers, the group of university-based writers such as Alfon, Bautista, Benitez, Arguilla to mention a few. These writers established the short story as a literary form par excellence for Filipino writers.

Furthermore, Lumbera (1997) mentions that by virtue of the writers' easy access to models, the writers set the pace in employing the form to tell about Philippine conditions although most of the works depict the lives of the middle class. Thus, Philippine fiction shows a desire to create a national literature in the hopes of defining the national psyche or identity of the Filipino. The table below shows the title, name and the birthplace of the authors of the materials under study.

Table 1. The novel and authors' place of origin

Title	Author
"Magnificence "	Estrella D. Alfon San Nicolas, Cebu City
"Of Fish, Flies, Dogs and	Timothy R. Montes

Women "	Borongan, Eastern, Samar
"The Chieftest Mourner"	Aida Rivera Ford Jolo, Sulu
"Thirsty is the Arid Land"	Liwayway Arceo-Bautista Manila
"The Wedding Dance"	Amador Daguio Laoag, Ilocos, Norte

It can be noted that the authors came from different regions of the country. Hence, although they are university-groomed writers, their genre still speak of their respective culture.

The phenomenology of human action lies on the worldview of human desire, yet to be satisfied by the idea of belongingness and acceptance in the community. The recognition of one's role is dependent of his/her culture. With that view, culture needs to be treated as an important factor in the shaping of society since it determines the expected behavior and norms of the people. This paper wants to discuss the underlying factors behind the concept of male and female societal roles in the Philippines as a result of cultural disparity among regions.

FRAMEWORK

Machismo is one of the most compelling reasons of infidelity as revealed in the 2001 study of Dr. Sandra Tempongko of the UP College of Public Health entitled "Determinants of Risky Behavior Related to Sexually Transmitted Diseases (STD's) Among Population Groups" as cited by Lee-Brago (2001). The study showed that infidelity happens during drinking sprees and through peer pressure. Drinking sprees are the common form of entertainment and 'bonding" among Filipino men which presumably proves their prowess and toughness as men.

What then is the counterpart role dictated by social norms for women? The above discussion of machismo signifies maternalism for Filipina women. Maternalism may be strengthened by another cliché, "Mother knows best," which refers to the mother's unquestionable instinct as a mother. Thus, maternalism refers to such precious acts of a mother to show her love, care, and affection among others, for the sake of her child/children.

Apparently, gender roles of both men and women are based on what the society expects them to do. One of the drives of the human person is the capability of feeling or having emotions, with the desire as one of them. Desire is a sense of longing for a person or object; it also refers to a person's hoping for a favorable outcome. Desire is also manifested in human feelings like "craving" or "hankering". When a person desires something or someone, his or her sense of longing is excited by the enjoyment or the thought of an object or person; in consequence, he or she expresses the want to take actions to satisfy his or her desire. The motivational aspect of desire has long been noted by philosophers like Thomas Hobbes, who asserts that human desire is the fundamental motivation of all human action.

Desire, as a literary theme, is at the core of literary genres all around the world particularly romantic novels such as *Madame Bovary* by Gustave Flaubert, *Gone with the Wind* by Margaret Mitchell and *Jane Eyre* by Charlotte Bronte. These works highlight how human desire is impeded by social conventions, class, or cultural barriers. The same theme is also manifested in gothic works such as *Dracula* by Bram Stoker, The *Phantom of the Opera* by Gaston Leroux, and *The Hunchback of Notre Dame* by Victor Hugo. In these works, desire is mingled with fear and dread. Poets like Homer and Edgar Allan Poe also deal with the themes of desire in their works.

Just as desire is central to the written fiction genre of romance, it is also the central theme in the contemporary Filipino films and soap operas such as *No Other Woman, Secret Affair, The Mistress,* and the recently-concluded telenovela, *The Legal Wife.* These works employ plots that appeal to the heightened emotions of the audience by showing "crises of human emotion, failed romance or friendship" in which desire is thwarted or unrequited

OBJECTIVES OF THE STUDY

This paper's point of contention focused on how infidelity is reflected and played in the works of fiction, particularly short stories. The author sought to loosen the tie that binds the origin of the act and understand fully the concept based on the gender roles played by the characters in selected works. Specifically, this paper aimed to study how the manifestation of culture and the inherent universal concept of desire are depicted as justification to the existence of

machismo and maternalism in the Philippines as depicted in the five selected short stories.

METHODOLOGY

The study is qualitative in nature adopting literary criticism as means of analysis. This paper employed Sigmund Freud's contention that the stuff of literature is the unresolved conflicts that give rise to any neurosis. Freud says of neurosis as the internal battle between the unconscious and the subconscious mind. Thus, he believes that a work of literature is the external expression of the author's unconscious mind. Accordingly, some Philippine short stories in English such as those used in this paper manifest Freud's concept of literature.

Another important consideration for this study was Hans–Georg Gadamer's viewpoint of hermeneutics. Gadamer believes that it is always important to consider descriptive phenomenology, in which he posits that understanding is related to the readers' encounter and the participation in a cultural tradition. Skinner (1985) explains further that, for Gadamer, understanding is not a matter of forgetting our own horizon of meanings but it is of merging or fusing our own horizon with the alien text or the alien society.

The analysis employed on the materials used in this study was both descriptive and contextual. Materials used were selected Philippine short stories in English which identify varying forms of machismo and maternalism. The authors' background as well as the development of Philippine literature in English was also considered.

RESULTS AND DISCUSSION

Analysis of the stories used in this paper revealed that the facets of machismo and maternalism can be traced back to desire. In Estrella Alfon's *Magnificence*, maternalism is seen in the mother of the two children. She is alert that she catches what Vicente is about to do to the innocent little girl. Had the mother not intervened, Vicente could have molested the little girl. Vicente's act exemplifies an extreme type of machismo.

Freud's tripartite model of the psyche has three parts such as id, ego and the superego. What Freud calls as pleasure principle drives one to seek pleasure and to avoid pain. The id is responsible for our basic drives such as food, sex and aggressive impulses, and demands immediate satisfaction. As for Vicente, his is obviously demonstrated when he is able to consume his desire for a girl of seven by kissing her during the tutorials; in addition, Vicente's id becomes strong towards the end of the story when he desires to do the molestation even more thinking that no one is around. He uses the pencils to lure the girl into his lap because he knows that she is fond of them. Children want to have pencils for their immediate satisfaction and be the envy of their peers.

The ego, which is the rational, logical, waking part of the mind, operates in harmony with the reality principle. Its main concern then is an individual's safety; the ego allows some of the id's desire to be expressed. The mother's superego shields her daughter from the pedophiled instincts that she thinks drives Vicente. Phallic symbols refer to the male generative powers. In *Magnificence*, the phallic symbol used is the pencil. Children love pencils, and they are crazy about them, so Vicente uses this object to seek pleasure with the girl. The two children use their possession of these pencils to brag to other kids at school. The colors of the pencil that Vicente gives to the children also have significance in the story. The girl receives red and yellow small pencils and a white jumbo–sized one. Red represents power/passion and sexuality, yellow means intelligence and consciousness, and white, being the biggest among the three, means innocence and purity/cleanliness. This is symbolic of the little girl, innocent and yet uncorrupted. She does not have dirty thoughts inside her mind so she does not show any consternated look as Vicente gains pleasure from "tutoring" her. The little girl does not see malice or lust in Vicente's overtures, given her state of innocence.

When the mother finds out what Vicente has been doing to her daughter, she simply asks her to leave. After showing her "magnificent" behavior towards Vicente, hence driving the man away into the darkness, the mother asks her daughter to take a bath quickly. Reminded of what she has seen, she presides over the bath that the girl takes, scrubs her with soap, and washes her with the hope of preserving the little girl's purity. In addition, she clothes the girl with new clothes and burns the old ones the girl was wearing before she discovered Vicente's despicable act. This bath that the mother gives her daughter symbolizes cleanliness and purity, to wash away the "stains" of Vicente's corrupting desire.

In Timothy Montes', *Of Flies, Fish, Dogs and Women,* the narrator, Maria has no choice but to sell fish to accomplish her role as mother and, to feed her five children amid the miserable condition of being a battered wife. Her maternalism is obvious in the desire to support the family and make up for the husband's irresponsibility so as to be able to provide for the family's needs. Maternalism is

also shown by another woman in the story. Angelica has no chance to help Maria from the dogs because she holds her baby in her arms. Maria advises Angelica to be brave for the sake of her baby and in the same way she regains her wits not to allow her husband to beat her again. The said situation adheres to the idea of Carl Jung which states that people from all over the world respond to certain situations because lying deep in their collective unconscious are the racial memories of humanity's past.

The husband, despite being an irresponsible head of the family asserts his machismo when he beats up his wife after getting intoxicated and losing his money on tuba and cockfighting. To cover his irresponsibility, the husband deliberately shows machismo through his barbaric and savage actions, beating up his wife so he could let people see that though the wife supports the family he still has the power over her.

In *The Chieftest Mourner*, the legal wife shows a different level and form of maternalism. In the absence of her own child, Sophia demonstrates protective instincts when she never allows the niece to "taste her uncle's lemonade." She even washes the inside of her niece's mouth with soap and water and calls upon at least a dozen of the saints to witness the act. There is an obvious purpose of hiding "grown-up" stories from the niece when the conversation between Sophia and the narrator's mother suddenly switches to Spanish. Sophia might have considered that exposure of ideas about the other woman named Esa, is not healthy for an eleven-year-old girl.

The machismo on the part of the poet may be seen in his action when he is tied to a chair with a strong rope after going home drunk. He walks out of the door, leaves his wife, never comes back, and eventually finds contentment in the arms of another woman. In his study about "The Unfaithful Husband- What Made Him Do It," Torento (1987) summarizes some of the cases of male infidelity from a marriage-and-family center and records of legal separation cases. Some of the reasons are the perception of lack of care and concern by the wife, pressures about providing for a domineering wife, all true in the case of the poet in the story.

In *Thirsty Is the Arid Land,* the daughter narrates how her mother suppresses her emotions. The aspect of maternalism in contrast with the machismo is presented by the mother when she does not express her pain and bitterness in front of her daughter even if the daughter knows the truth. This action intends to maintain the reputation of the father in the daughter's eyes. The father exhibits machismo by being a good provider for the family and hides the proof of his affair in the "pink box" which both the daughter and the mother eventually and inadvertently discover. The story is set in a milieu in which Filipinos' culture was focused on the family orientation with stereotypical gender roles of the parents and the child/children.

Along with the cultural tradition principle, *Awiyao,* in *The Wedding Dance*, has to leave *Lumnay* and must marry *Madulinay* because of his desire to have a child. He decides to do so after receiving ridicule and pressure from the other males of their tribe since he has not had a child with Lumnay after seven harvests. In one of Awiyao's lines to Lumnay, he says, "You know that life is not worth living without a child." That statement proves Alano's (1995) report that five of the six highest probable reasons for a husband's infidelity are related to marital and family dissatisfaction. These include lousy marriage, neglect of kids/ household duties, neglect of the spouse, and not having children. Considering *Wedding Dance,* the fifth reason justifies Awiyao's decision to leave Lumnay and attempt to marry Madulinay instead. When Lumnay lets go of Awiyao, she gets to show her selfless love towards her husband, which is her maternalism. From the study of Gonzales (1991), the sources of resilience for the Filipino wife are varied: faith, prayer, religion, friends and family, professional counsellors and psychiatrists, priests, education, work and personal care. In the case of *Lumnay* her maternalism is the love she definitely expresses for husband. Maternalism can be applied to anyone referring to the quality of having or showing the tenderness, warmth, and affection towards others.

The characters in the works of fiction under study who exhibit respective gender roles are representation of male and female in the society where they be- long. This paper utilized primarily the idea of Freud focusing on his concept of literature as the expression of author's unconscious mind. Likewise, the analysis also limits the hermeneutics of Gadamer to the understanding of the text emphasizing that the reader's understanding is basically rooted from his/her cultural background. This paper does not involve other types of hermeneutics such as of Heidegger and other psychoanalytic issues of Jung.

CONCLUSIONS

Machismo and maternalism though they vary depending on given situations, are simply the result of one's adherence to social norms which a man or a woman does not desire to change for fear of being criticized. There are different forms and range of reasons that a person may provide to justify his/her compliance with

these norms. Such occurrences may be understood by another individual if he or she takes into account his or her personal perspective of life. Faithfulness and infidelity are the same with the different perception of human senses; accordingly, gender roles are subsequent to the culture and origin of people. As manifested in the short stories considered for this paper, desire can be viewed as the root of gender roles. In a similar way, Filipinos' concept of gender roles is rooted from their cultural and religious upbringing tainted by the society's expectations.

RECOMMENDATIONS

The researcher recommends that in reading, analyzing or teaching literature, one must consider the background of the text, such as the authors' background, time of writing and the eminent theme of the period unless otherwise employing the New Criticism type, or the "Isolationist." In the case of Philippine literature, one must consider that it can be understood and interpreted in the context of history. The two major colonial aggressions (Spanish and American) set as strands that influence regional and ethnic differences but somehow comprise the common theme of Philippine literature.

Furthermore, it is suggested to consider the use of four reality frames in teaching literature such as; literature as history, art, aesthetic and script. With those, understanding of the text shall be in accordance to Gadamer's "fusion of horizon."

LITERATURE CITED

Alano, M. 1995 "Infidelity: The Dynamics of the Querida System in the Philippines. A Dissertation, Faculty of the Graduate School. Ateneo de Manila Univer- sity. Retrieved on January 25, 2013 from http://goo.gl/l7F2E4

Bressler, C. E. 1999 "Literary Criticism, An Introduction to Theory and Practice Second edition: Prentice hall Inc. New Jersey, USA. Retrieved on January 23, 2013 from http://goo.gl/3ayfLM

Gonzales, T. 1991 "House Bill No. 3502 "Revised Penal Code." Retrieved on January 24, 2013 from http://www.congress.gov.ph/download/

Lee-Brago, P. 2001 Why Pinoy (Filipino) Men Cheat their Wives. Retrieved on January 23, 2013 from http://www.philstar.com/philstar/News200104029927193. htm

Lumbera, B. 1997 Revaluation 1997 *Essays on Philippine Literature, Cinema and Popular Culture*, UST, Manila, Philippines.

Skinner, Q. (Ed.). 1990 *The return of grand theory in the human sciences*. Cambridge University Press.

CHAPTER 2

Structural and Motifemic Analysis of Legends

Published in Journal of International Academic Research for Multidisciplinary

ISSN: 2320-5083, Volume 6, Issue 1, February 2018

ABSTRACT

Legends are fully formed narratives that are considered recapitulations of past experiences, showcasing the identity of a people. With this concept, this research analyzed said indigenous materials to uncover the identity of the people to whom the legends belong. It attempted to study the classification, structure and themes of the legends of Sorsogon City and their variants. The results emphasize the difference between the prose narratives from fiction, having its own distinct elements. This is an interpretative type of literary criticism. After the data collection, validation were done simultaneously using the parameters of Manuel's vertical and horizontal tests. Through the structural and motifemic analysis of the legends, the study revealed that there are beliefs, traits, values traditions and cultural practices reflected therein. It was recommended to undertake similar studies on legends or other prose narratives of other provinces/ regions/ nations to understand better the humanity of the people to whom the said genre belongs thereby preserving them for posterity.

Keywords- Legends, Literary Criticism, Motifemic Analysis, Sorsogon City, Bicol Region, Philippines

INTRODUCTION

One of the fundamental objectives of education is to perpetuate all that is desirable in our national heritage. It aims to awaken awareness and appreciation for the uniqueness of our identity as a people, and take pride in the legacy our forebearers have bequeathed. If Rizal envisioned the youth to carry on the torch of progress for the fatherland, then it is through what they learn today about the past, that will determine what they make of the future. Education must provide a panoramic view of a country's continuing saga not only by means of written history but also through oral and unrecorded indigenous practices of its people. Philippine educators are now cognizant of this growing need, that they have been encouraging "field studies" on regional literature; hence more materials on our culture should be included in the curriculum.

The researcher opines that every person should have a better understanding of his cultural heritage, its belief, customs and traditions. Thus, being a teacher, she should know the nature of the learner in order to provide concept/ideas applicable to his needs. In the same sense, the learner should also be aware of his own nature to know himself better, leading him to an understanding of his ways as well as that of others particularly those of the same community where he belongs.

Folklore, is commonly defined as the "lore of the folk; the knowledge of the people". It is a new terminology which took the place of the phrase "popular antiquities that include old beliefs, customs, superstitions and sayings of the people. It was coined in 1846 by an English antiquary William John Thomas. The different genres of folklore such as myths, epics and legends serve as a showcase depicting people's culture and tradition. Hence these genres are effective vehicles in explaining and/or validating the nature of an individual in relation to his ethnic group.

Despite the significance of such folkloric genres to our cultural identity, it is sad to note that researchers in Bicol Folklore are bothered by the dearth of published materials in indigenous lore all over the region. Not much focus is given to these folkloric items that abound in the different provinces of Bicol; particularly on Sorsoguenos' verbal - prose tradition.

Sorsogon City, being the first and only city in the province of Sorsogon was chosen as the locale of the study because of various considerations. It is one of the seven cities in the Region V or known as Bicol Region consists of six provinces such as Albay, Camarines Norte, Camarines Sur, Catanduanes, Masbate and Sorsogon. Its geographical location presents a center of trade, commerce, industry and education. It has a rustic ambiance which combines with its rural and cosmopolitan outlook. The population of the locale is composed of Sorsoguenos from other municipalities of the province as well as migrants from Bicol and other regions. They carry with them non-material components of their culture such as language, customs and traditions, beliefs, values and other forms of verbal traditions. Though legends abound in the rural-urban city of Sorsogon, very little has been done by way of collecting and compiling genre for posterity.

The researcher has decided to undertake the task to explore and uncover the vast wealth of 'legendary treasure" this study hoped to yield. This study focused on the collected, transcribed and translated Sorsogon legends and attempted to analyze their nature, role and function to society, Specifically, it sought answers to the following: what typology/classification are drawn from the identified legends; what beliefs, traits, values, traditions and cultural practices are reflected in the legends; and what instructional materials out of the legends can be proposed in teaching English and Philippine literature?

THEORETICAL BACKGROUND

This study was anchored on several theories on the reciprocal nature of a society's culture and literature/folklore in relation to community identity. According to Goldstein (1964) "every society creates its own culture and literature". It is supported by the idea of Maramba (1940) who claims that "for while a literature disseminates itself, it simultaneously disseminates the culture behind it". The study of culture and literature prove to be beneficial if one wants to know the background of a particular society. In the local setting, it can be noted that it is incumbent upon every Bikolano to involve himself in the further retrieval or collection and study of Bikol. This action may help the Sorsoguenos find the roots of his abundant and meaningful culture, to explain his present dream, aspirations, heartaches and cope with worries and problems to finally find his suitable and valuable position in the future

Folklore, one of the oldest forms of literature is a product of culture and society. It serves as a showcase of the earliest forms of literature such as myths, legends, tales, proverbs, riddles, songs and dance forms which are transmitted from one generation to another. The different folkloric genres of Sorsogon City once collected, translated, documented, classified as folklore and analyzed according to their narrative elements uncovered some of the traits, practices, culture and traditions that the present generation should get to know and understand.

According to Bernabe, Bonifacio and Tangco (2001), "It is reasonable to say that folklore, legends in particular shared by Filipinos is a vital part of Philippine culture, thus legends served both as an "integrative and substantial" part of the Sorsoguenos' culture. Integrative in the sense that it is a medium that unifies and binds the members of the community in words and deeds. It is also substantial because it is the articulation of beliefs, concepts and practices that serve as identity which also promote social and cultural awareness and concern.

MATERIALS AND METHODS

The primary sources of data were legends collected from the informants of the different barangays in Sorsogon City who were instrumental in the validation of said data as folkloric materials. During the collection of legends, the researcher simultaneously conducted the vertical and horizontal tests of Manuel (1967) to validate the folkloricity and authenticity of each item. The two contexts of folklore research and collection were considered- the natural and artificial context as cited and used by Segundoi in the methodology of her work. The said contexts were discussed by Goldstein in his book, A Guide to Field Workers on Folklore.

This paper used an interpretative type of literary criticism. It employed the content analysis under the descriptive method which aims to the objective, systematic and qualitative description of the manifest content of communication as discussed by Aquino (1977). The collected and translated legends were classified according to types. Structural and motifemic analysis highlighting the form, nature, role and function of the legend was further undertaken to determine the motifs which in turn formulate the theme/themes of the narrative.

RESULTS AND DISCUSSIONS

There is a total of fifty-three (53) identified legends of Sorsogon City categorized into three. The first classification, Origin of Names of Places, has thirty-nine (39) legends with nine (9) variants; the second classification, Origin of Geographical Location or Landmarks, has three (3) legends and one (1) variant The third classification, Origin of a Plant, has only one (1) legend and no available variant.

Of the three classifications of Sorsogon City legends, the greatest number are on names of places, and such have been influences by previous colonizers (Spaniards, Japanese, Americans) who had occupied the place, mingled and familiarized themselves with the native inhabitants; as well as the local customs and traditions of the people. Likewise, miscommunication on the part of the colonizer and the local inhabitants due to language confusion also led to naming of certain places.

Variants of the Identified Legends

Variants are versions of the same text that have some (minor) contradictions to other types but they neither carry different messages nor represent possible changes of mind on the part of the narrator and his audience. The legends have been passed on from generations by word of mouth and in the course of transmission, some details might have been omitted consciously or unconsciously while others could have been added due to the imagination or enthusiasm of the story teller, hence the presence of variants.

Each narrator or story teller has his/her own unique/individual style of narrating a story. Some are meticulous enough to include each and every detail of the narrative, while others only focus on the main point or gist of the story.

Narrative Structure:

After the legends were validated and considered as authentic folkloric materials, each item was analyzed based on the elements of folklore as prose narratives. The principal elements are orientation, complicating action and the resolution/result. However, Labov (1972) also takes into consideration the addition of the abstract or summary, evaluation and coda whatever the analysis requires it. The researcher included a synthesis of each structural analysis to determine the main subject/idea of the entire narrative. It also explains the reason/s why or how a particular legend came about.

Abstract is the entire idea or summary of the narrative. This is often followed by the orientation except when the evaluation comes after it. This element, however, is not present in other patterns if the orientation comes first in the narrative.

Orientation refers to the time, place, characters involved and situation in which the events of a narrative occur. This is always present in the combination of elements except in an abstract-evaluation pattern.

Complicating action is the structuring of the relationship between characters and events. It is the highest point of Interest or the turning point in the story. This is always followed by either the resolution/result or evaluation.

Evaluation is the perception of the outcome based on the given situation/conflict as described in the narrative. It may come before or after the resolution/result. Its position varies depending on the manner of narration used by the informant.

Resolution/result is the culmination of the narrative which shows whether or not the problem is resolved. It is present in nine, out of eleven patterns and its order in the structural chronology can be interchanged with the evaluation.

Coda signals the end of the narrative. This is often added in narratives to emphasize the belief in supernatural powers and the will of the Supreme Being.

Pattern of Elements in the Narrative

Legends follow a particular pattern of elements in revealing the facts/ideas in the narrative. There were eleven (11) patterns such as:

a. abstract-orientation-complicating action-resolution/result-coda
b. abstract-orientation-complicating action-resolution/result
c. abstract-orientation-evaluation
d. abstract-evaluation
e. orientation-complicating action-evaluation- resolution/result-coda
f. orientation-complicating action-resolution/result-coda
g. orientation-complicating action-evaluation-resolution/result
h. orientation-complicating action-resolution/result
i. orientation-resolution/result-evaluation
j. orientation-complicating action-resolution/result-evaluation
k. orientation-evaluation

The stories related b) the informants in the vernacular were recorded and translated faithfully to the "original text" as possible without in any way altering any of the details or sequence of narration. Based on the combinations arrived at after the structural analysis, it can be deduced that legends follow any of the eleven (11) individual patterns in revealing the idea or essence of the narrative. The presence of one element compliments another, but the absence of one does not necessarily affect the meaning of the whole. Each element has its own function different from the other depending on the given information and on the manner of narration rendered by the informant.

The structural patterns of legends are dependent upon its narrator. All the elements of a prose narrative may or may not be present in the rendering of a story. Some may lack one, two, three or four of said elements but the main idea or essence of the narrative is not in any way altered nor affected. The completeness or incompleteness of the narrative based on the combination of elements is largely dependent upon the circumstances of narration. Unlike the short story and other written prose types which are fixed forms, the legend which is oral in origin has a flexible structural pattern dependent upon its narration.

Of the filly-three (53) legends including the existing variants, one (1) each falls under the abstract-orientation-complicating action-resolution/result-coda; orientation-complicating action-evaluation-resolution/result-coda and orientation-resolution/result-evaluation patterns; two (2) each under the abstract-orientation-complicating action-resolution/result; orientation- complicating action-evaluation-result and orientation-complicating action-resolution/result-evaluation. Five (5) under the orientation-evaluation combination; six (6) under the abstract- orientation-evaluation; seven (7) under the orientation-complicating action-evaluation- resolution-coda; ten (10) under the orientation-complicating action-resolution/result, and sixteen (16) for the abstract-evaluation pattern.

Beliefs, Traits, Values, Traditions and Cultural Practices Reflected in Legends

The researcher divided the discussion into two. The first comprises the beliefs, traditions and cultural practices; and the second includes the traits and values discernible from the narratives.

A. Beliefs, Traditions and Cultural Practices

The Sorsoganons have particular beliefs, traits, positive and negative values, traditions and cultural practices that are discernible from the legends and are still observed up to the present.

1. Belief in the presence of evil spirits-

2. Belief that lightning could turn people or things into stones from the following legends;

3. Belief in Superstitions

4. Belief in punishment by the Supreme Being in the event that the children disobey their parents.

5. Belief in Miraculous Deeds of Patron Saints from the two legends:

6. Belief in the effect of curses.

7. The tradition of Bayanihan.

8. The Celebration of the Feast of Saints.

9. The practice of serenading a woman as a way of showing affection.

10. The practice of using fireworks during fiesta and merry-making activities.

Traits and Values

Both positive and negative traits and values of the people from the community where said legends originated were also taken into account.

Table 1 . Positive and Negative Traits and Values

Positive	Negative
1.Bravery/Courage	1.Envy
2.Friendliness	2. Impulsiveness
3.Generosity	3.Disobedience
4.Religiosity	4.Lack of Respect for Elders
5.Assertiveness/fighting one's right	for 5. Ignorance or lack of education
6.Unity	

Of the six (6) reflected positive values, religiosity was revealed in five (5) legends. This trait/values was considered the most common among others.

Bravery/courage stand second in the number of legends where this trait was reflected. Generosity, assertiveness and unity were in two (2) legends and friendliness is the trait reflected only in one.

Based from the number of legends where the above-mentioned traits and values where reflected, it can be deduced that Bicolanos, Sorsoguenos in particular are indeed religious. They are also brave and courageous whenever the situation calls for it.

In terms of negative traits and values, lack of education was depicted in five

(5) legends, mostly from the naming of places due to language confusion between the inhabitant and colonizer. Disobedience to parents was also reflected in four (4) legends where it can be traced from the old tradition that daughters should follow their parents' choice of husband. There were four (4) narratives reflecting envy and lack of respect and another legend that revealed impulsiveness of the characters.

It can be figured out from the discussion that lack of education and disobedience were the most common negative traits deduced from the narratives. However, although they have been considered as negative, it can be inferred that it was only because of the situation/condition stated in the story. Lack of education/ignorance is not an innate character of a person. The characters involved in the items where this trait was exhibited were only victims of circumstances. Similarly, disobedience was mostly displayed by characters who are daughters arranged to marry men, who are chosen by their parents.

CONCLUSIONS AND RECOMMENDATIONS

Legends are prose narratives regarded as true by the narrator and his audience. It is set in a period less remote when the world was such as it is today, and present a human situation from which a problem arises or is presented followed by its consequences or outcome. They also serve as a showcase and vehicles of the culture and identity of a people, as part of the expression through language. They function as basic to social tradition, which contribute part of the social heritage, or the "living mirrors of the past".

Based on the aforementioned findings, the researcher came up with the following conclusions: (1) The typology drawn from the legends of Sorsogon City include origin of names of places, origin of geographical features or landmarks and origin of a plant. (2) There are ten (10) variants from the total number of collected legends. Nine from origin of names of places and one from origin of geographical features or landmarks. (3) Legends are describable in terms of the five elements of prose narratives to determine structural patterns and motifemes. (4) Six beliefs such as the presence of evil spirits, lightning turning people or things into stone, superstition, punishment by the supreme Being, miraculous deeds of saints, and effect of curses were gleaned from the motifemes. Likewise, the tradition of bayanihan, the celebration of patron saints; the practice of serenading a woman: and using fireworks during fiesta or merry making activities were other evident practices revealed. Six positive and five negative traits were also reflected from said legends. Local legends can also be used as instructional materials in teaching.

The researcher recommends the following on the basis of the preceding conclusions:

(1) Undertake similar studies on legends or other prose narratives of other provinces/regions and even other nation to understand better the humanity of the people to whom these prose narratives belong; and for comparative studies with other places having the same folkloric genre; (2) Include local legends and other types of prose narratives in the study of Bicol literature and introduce various folkloric methods of analysis according to the specific indigenous genre; (3) Incorporate Sorsogon prose narratives particularly legends into the curriculum of Philippine Literature subjects in different schools of Sorsogon Province; (4) Initiate compilations and publications of other types of Sorsogon prose narratives and of other provinces and region for posterity; and (5) Use the reflected traits and values from the local legends to enhance/develop , enrich or re direct the present generation's way of life.

REFERENCES

Aquino,G.V. 1977. Quezon City Philippines, Alemar-Phoenix Publishing House, Philippines.

Bernabe, Bo.nifacio and Tangco. 2001 :Social Science Information, A Special Issue on Folklore: UP Folklorist Series, Vol. No. 1 June-July.

Goldstein,K. 1964. A Guide for Field Workers in Folklore,: Hatboro: Folklore Associate.

Labov, W. 1972. Language in the Inner City; University of Pennsylvania Press, Philadelpia.

Manuel,A. 1967. "The Study of Philippine Folklore" in Brown Heritage, Antonio Manuel ed. , Quezon City, Ateneo De Manila University Press, Manila.

Maramba,A.D.ed. 1971. Early Philippine Literature from Ancient Times to 1940 ; Malabon, Manila, Philippines.

CHAPTER 3

Grotesque Motifs in Classical Literature as Motives of Millennials'' Affection to Scary Stories

Published in Research Journal of English Language and Literature (RJELAL)

Pint ISSN:2395-2636 ; Online ISSN 2321-3108

ABSTRACT

Hornedo (1999) in his essay, Conceptual Structure of the Relationship of Theory to Literary Text, explains that "the teacher is treating literature after a theory- his own theory, which is literature as a useful art. It is measured by its effects, and form is valued for what it can do for the sake of content". The said idea adheres to this study which explores the subversive undertow of the grotesque motifs from the classical type of literary material to the taste of the modern reader. The materials are considered good number of representative such as, Richard III, the creation of Dr. Frankenstein, Quasimodo, and Erik the Phantom. This paper intends to unravel reasons behind the strange affection of the Millenials to the literary works with deformed characters or scary themes. This paper uses a descriptive-qualitative type of research which anchors on the theories of the grotesque as an analytical tool to present the motives behind the Millenial's allure to the literary materials with scary or deformed characters. The discussion starts with the Theories of the Grotesque and follows four phases titled as: The Unmasking of the Faces; The Veiling of the Faces; the Damnation of the Faces; and The Readers' Attraction to the Faces. It is therefore encouraged that the teachers, being the basic facilitator of learning situation, should have a wide understanding of their learners' needs in terms of the materials that will be utilized in the process of presentation, discussion, and assimilation.

Keywords *– Grotesque, Classical Literature, Millennials*

INTRODUCTION

The reemergence of the grotesque in the arts was only one of a remarkable range of new expressive models through which the grotesque was extended, expanded, and reinvented in the nineteenth and twentieth centuries. These cultural vehicles for the grotesque included such disparate developments as psychoanalysis, photography, mass media, science fiction, ethnography, weapons of mass destruction, globalization, and virtual reality.

The modern era witnessed an explosion of literary imagery that in various ways incorporated grotesque. A remarkable number of canonical works of modernism, include motifs from classical literature. The Hunchback of Notre Dame by Victor Hugo, Cyrano de Bergerac by Edmond Rostand, Richard III by William Shakespeare, Wuthering Heightsby Emily Bronte, Jane Eyre by Charlotte, Jude the Obscure by Thomas Hardy, Le Fantome de L'Opera by Gaston Leroux, La Belle et la Bete first published version by Gabrielle-Suzanne Barbot de Villenueve, Frankenstein by Mary Shelley, and so much more, employ structures deeply rooted in the western tradition as grotesque. The grotesque characters are prominent in novels, short stories, poems, dramas, but it also plays a role even in creative non-fiction and the visual arts such as films and paintings.

Accordingly, the term Millenials, refer to the people who grew up in the turn of the 21st century. A Time Magazine article placed them to be born between1980-2000. Millenials are known to be flexible or tolerant of difference. Being born in the age of technological advancement with electronics- filled and rampant use of social media through the worldwide web, they are the generation that requires keen marketing attention. They are not easy to be pleased by a traditional way of presentation. Hence, some researches probe on their needs and interest.

The literary materials that get the most attention of most of the Millenials are those that are far from the ordinary. They love things that are different. In the research of Carretero, Gilbas and Remolacio(2011) on the Motivating situations in Reading, the scary stories ranked first as the top choice or preference of the respondents. Both the book and movie industry seem to address the inclination of the new generation to the idea of gothic. The common examples are the movies with the idea of deconstruction where the basic villain-type character becomes the hero /heroine. The examples of such are, Maleficent, Pan, Hanzel and Gretel, and Alice Through the Looking Glass, to mention some.

THEORETICAL BACKGROUND

The grotesque was first linked to the notion of "primitive" expression to other primal realities. In Le monster, published in 1889, where Huysman contended that the microscope revealed an entirely new field of monstrosities equal to any of those animating medieval art.Similarly, as explained in the Encyclopedia of Contemporary Literary Theory: Approaches, Scholars, Terms Contemporary, Frued'sexploration of the unconscious was embraced by surrealists who employed grotesque modalities Given the prominent role of the grotesque in modern image culture, there are surprisingly few significant studies on these issues, a failure that reveals a blind spot in art-history and practice. The neoclassical foundations of art history and aesthetics, with their emphasis on ideated beauty and rational inquiry, set up an intrinsic hostility toward grotesque. There is, however, an even unprecedented disjuncture and shifting boundaries, with the collision of cultures and scientific challenges repeatedly stripping away the veneer of familiar reality from the chaos of raw experience. The details lay down bare the answers to the mystery of the readers' attraction to the gothic and grotesque. They help clear out the invoking of sympathy to the characters presented.

Thus, this study explores the subversive undertow of the grotesque within the modern, with a good number of representatives as follows: Richard III, the creation of Dr. Frankenstein, Quasimodo, and Erik the Phantom.

The Theories of Grotesque

The chief difficulty encountered in seeking to define the grotesque in its relation to media is— as can be attested to by every theoretician who has sought to do so since the sixteenth century conception of the term in its modern sense—that the grotesque is not an expression of norms, but rather what results from the transgression of them. In recognition of the grotesque as the slipperiest of aesthetic qualities the flurry of nineteenth century writers addressing the grotesque did so by exploring its aesthetic, social and philosophical significance.

Theoretical attempts to iron down the meaning and implications of the grotesque have addressed it alternately as a quality of media or as a quality of interaction with media, or even alternatively as a quality of the act of mediation itself. As a quality of media the grotesque has proven particularly susceptible to the conceptual fluctuations of history.

Kayser,(1981) the father of modern grotesque theory, identifies the definition of the term as the central issue in the study of it, assessing it himself as the appearance of a reality that is simultaneously of and opposed to the worlds in which its audience take part. Kayser's focus on definition is not novel, but the direction from which he approaches the issue is.

Harpham (1976) summarizes the approach in his presentation of the effective standard, a standard based in the temporality of grotesque form versus the fairly constant evocative effect it has historically had upon the viewer and in his own assertion that "Etymological consistency does not equal conceptual accuracy." For Harpham, this effect is the establishment through the grotesque of a structure of estrangement, separated from the completely fantastic by the maintenance of the reality of the world while deconstructing the illusion of its basic reliability.

Objectives

This paper aims to enlighten the reasons behind the sweeping, fantastic stories that evoke concepts through history and literature. The outcast, the mythology of beauty and the beast, the use of masks, the society, and the power of literature are the main subjects of discussion. This paper intends to present motives to the ideas and language which seem dry and dull at first glance but later come vividly to life on pages. Furthermore, this work aims to identify the reasons behind the strange affection of the Millenials to the literary works with deformed characters or scary themes.

METHODOLOGY

This paper uses a descriptive- qualitative type of research which anchors on the theories of the grotesque as an analytical tool to present the motives behind the Millenial's allure to the literary materials with scary or deformed characters. The materials include written forms such as novels and play, but not limited to the visual type or the films. This paper's materials focus on the four representative of classical literature, Richard III by William Shakespeare, Frankenstein by Mary Shelley, The Hunchback of Notre Dame by Victor Hugo, and Le Fantome de L'Opera by Gaston Leroux. The primary basis of selecting the materials is the presence the main character with physical deformity. They are also considered as classic type of literature, famous and still recognized in the contemporary time.

The discussion follows four phases titled as: The Unmasking of the Faces, where the characters in each genre are described; The Veiling of the Faces, which uncovers the type of personality and the reason why they became physically ugly; the Damnation of the Faces which discusses the societal culture that are reflected in the stories; and The Readers' attraction to the Faces. The discussion of the Theories of the

Grotesque serves as a background information for deeper understanding and easy grasp of this paper's point of contention.

RESULTS AND DISCUSSION

The Unmasking of the Faces

A. Richard III – Richard III William Shakespeare, printed in 1597; Performed between 1600-1601) He is also called the duke of Gloucester,

and eventually crowned King Richard III. He has a deformed body and twisted mind. He is both the central character and the villain of the play. He is evil, corrupt, sadistic, and manipulative, and he will stop at nothing to become king. His intelligence, political brilliance, and dazzling use of language keep the audience fascinated—and his subjects and rivals under his thumb.

B. Frankenstein Creation - Frankenstein (Mary Shelley , 1818)

Victor Frankenstein's creation is often referred to as the monster. He is roughly eight feet tall, hideously ugly creation assembled from old body parts and strange chemicals, animated by a mysterious spark. He has watery yellow eyes and a withered, translucent yellowish skin that barely conceals the muscular system and blood vessels. Oddly, the creature has perfect, white teeth, black lips and long black hair. He has the strength of a giant, yet an infant mind. He has a gentle nature, yet his physical defects hide his goodness and make everyone fear and mistreat him.

The monster tries to integrate himself into society, only to be shunned universally. Looking in the mirror, he realizes his physical grotesqueness, an aspect of his persona that blinds society to his initially gentle, kind nature. And Victor feels unmitigated hatred for his creation, the monster shows that he is not a purely evil being. The monster's eloquent narration of events (as provided by Victor) reveals his remarkable sensitivity and benevolence. He assists a group of poor peasants and saves a girl from drowning, but because of his outward appearance, he is rewarded only with beatings and disgust.

C. Quasimodo - The Hunchback of Notre Dame (Victor Hugo, 1831)

Quasimodo is the abandoned child left at Notre Dame and adopted by Archdeacon Claude Frollo. Hideously deformed, he has a giant humpback, a protrusion coming out of his chest, and a giant wart that covers one of his eyes. He is also deaf. His heart is pure, and this purity is linked to the cathedral itself. Indeed, his love for Notre Dame's bells and for the beautiful sound of their ringing represents his only form of communication. The whole of Paris ironically enjoys his "singing" while at the same time detesting him for his ugliness. His name literally means "half-made".

D. Erik - Le Fantome de L'opera(Gaston Leroux, 1909-1910)

He was born near Rouen in France, and ran away from home at a young age because his parents were horrified by him, his own father never seeing his face. He travelled Europe with the freak shows, being displayed as the Living Corpse, and singing with unearthly beauty, learning magic tricks from the gypsies. Tales of his skills went with the traders who saw him, and reached the court of the Sultan in Persia.

Erik is a genius of music but always wears a mask because of his ugly appearance. His frightening look scared everyone. People thought of him as a ghost haunted in the opera house. He has a devil's appearance but an angel's voice. He lives underneath the Paris Opera House with a lonely heart because he was abandoned by his parents with no place to go.

The Veiling of the Faces

A. Richard III

In the first scene of the first act Richard III is already seen regarding his despicable appearance with self-pity. He further justifies that since he cannot be a lover then he chooses to be a villain. From here it is made clear that his physical deformity has caused him a lot of misery and insecurity, that the hatred that he feels for others, members of his family, and himself is deeply rooted and primarily caused by his appearance.

His deformity also makes it impossible to attain the love of Lady Anne, the young widow of Prince Edward (whose death, as well as the death of all the other Lancasters is brought upon them by Richard's hand) who is utterly repulsed by him and tells him so in the next scene wherein she expresses her repulsion by calling him a string of names: "fiend conjured up by a black magician" (L. 34-35), "foul devil" (L.50), "thou lump of foul deformity" (L.57). Although at the end of the second scene in the first act Richard has a momentary boost of confidence and is taken over by the illusion that he is good- looking caused by Lady Anne's acceptance, arguably feigned as it was, of his love.

B. Frankenstein's Creation

Victor Frankenstein's fascination in the mystery of the creation of life led him in the study of how human body is built and how it falls apart, and goes one step further: discovering the secret of life. He works months on his creation from human corpse pieces but when he brings it to life, its awful appearance horrifies him. The "monster" is rejected by his own creator because of his hideous looks. People who saw him were horrified and drove him away. Reflecting on his own situation, he realizes that he is deformed, horribly different from human beings and alone.

Society cannot accept his horrible appearance and so he decided to find refuge and solitude in the wilderness. His unearthly ugliness rendered it almost too horrible for human eyes. Victor curses him and drives him away when they met.

The monster's growing understanding of the social significance of family is connected to his sense of otherness and solitude. Observing the kindness and devotion to each other of the DeLaceys family, causes the monster to suffer as he realizes how truly alone and how far from being the recipient of such kindness. The lack of interaction with others, in addition to his namelessness, compounds the monster's woeful lack of social identity.

The monster tells a sad and moving story about how he has been alienated from the world (being a corpse-parts conglomeration can do that to you), and how he killed the boy out of revenge. The monster asks Victor to create for him a female companion as monstrous as him when he learns about the pleasures and obligations of the family and of human relations in general, which deepens the agony of his own isolation.

C. Quasimodo

Being an infant, he was abandoned by his own mother and when given over to the church at Notre Dame, no one adopts him, thus Claude Frollo one of the priests declares to raise the misshapen baby. The churchwomen, who have always championed the cause of abandoned babies and found suitable homes for them, proclaim him to be the devil.

His appearance, which seems to be almost half-beast and half-human is a perfect and exaggerated example of ugliness. His hunched back, one-eyed and disfigured face makes the citizens of Paris think he is evil. Nobody other than Frollo speaks with him. He takes the responsibility of ringing the bells of the cathedral which eventually causes his deafness. He considers the bells as his friends having no one else to talk to (aside from Frollo) and endures the insults and accusations of the people of Paris. This makes him feels sad, isolated and lonely. However, he feels totally rejected when his own beloved master ignores his needs.

D. Erik

"The Phantom's" distorted personalities attributes to different underlying factors. Nobody wants to get along with him in his childhood. Even his parents hate and ignore him. Other children tease him and make a fool of him while the adults think he is a devil which brings bad luck to them. Being deserted, he develops sense of inferiority and chooses to close his heart and live alone in the darkness. Aware of his horrifying appearance that may scare Christine, he hides behind and pretends to be "an angel of music"

Erik is a tortured soul, a mind and heart in agony. He's wounded and broken within, but radiates a hardened exterior to mask his pain. No one gives him compassion, and as a result his heart has become dark and angry. He lives a life in isolation, hidden in the shadows, and untouched by the warmth of another human being. He is unloved and unwanted. He dreams of beauty and secretly yearns for heaven, but lives in perpetual hell. He hates who he is, a gargoyle of a man doomed to a life of loneliness.

He wants his girl, Christine, to love the monster behind the mask. He longs to be loved for who he truly is. When his desire for being loved was not attained, he thoughtthat no one truly accept him and became desperate to be freed from his lonely existence.His face reflects the two warring personalities that dwell within him -- light and darkness; yet his personality still cries for redemption.

The Damnation of the Faces

The common aspect of rejection and reason of the society's disapproval of the characters such as Richard III, Frankenstein's creation, Quasimodo and Erik is the rule of the binary. Light and dark, beautiful and ugly, bad and evil. People always associate the ugly to the dark and evil side. Having physical deformities and monstrosities, those characters are rejected and condemned. It is regardless of how compassionate they are internally, their external features devoid them of people's approval or acceptance.

Grotesque describes the aberration from ideal form and from accepted convention, to create the misshapen, ugly, exaggerated, or even formless. This type runs the extentof deliberate exaggerations of caricature, to the unintended abnormalities, accidents, and failures of the everyday world represented in realistic imagery, to the dissolution of bodies, forms, and categories.

While gaps, or disunities, of the combinatory and aberrant grotesques requires an imaginative leap, the metamorphic grotesque does much of this work for the readers. This grotesque can combine or deform in the same way as its static counterparts, but the metamorphic exists in the process, the "morphing" from one thing or form to another. It also seems much more reliant on mimesis and illusion, transgressing them for its impact. (Connely, 2003)

Central to the grotesque is its lack of fixity, its unpredictable and its instability. Victor Hugo's observation has special resonance here: that ideal beauty has only one standard whereas the variations and combinations possible for the grotesque are limitless. A premise central to Kant's idea of the beautiful, that it makes us feel as though the world is purposive, that it is here for us, cannot be more brutally and specifically refuted than in the disfigured humans playing a game of chance.

The Readers' Attraction to the Faces

The personalities of those figures make the readers empathize and sympathize with them. Each of the featured characters has a quality that may redeem the deformity in their appearances. In the narratives, those characters suffer from maltreatment, rejection and betrayal of people around them, making them seek for revenge or eventually secluding themselves.

Despite Richard's deformities, he has brilliance with words and his persuasive emotional manipulations fascinates the" readers. The Creation of Frankenstein or "The Monster" has a complex duality which is evident in his actions. He has the great desire for companionship, a kind and pure heart at the beginning despite of his physical monstrosity. However, he also seeks for revenge and turns him to be a killer due to the rejection against his existence.

Quasimodo breaks the heart of the reader through his fascinating personality amidst his physical ugliness. His sense of loyalty and faithfulness to his master and unconditional love to Esmeralda are enough qualities that may divert the readers' attention and feel sympathy towards him. Eric or The Phantom in a way resembles the character of Quasimodo, being despised by his own parents and abandoned by the society. However, his desire to be loved is quite similar to the creation of Frankenstein who wishes for companionship. Every reader may feel compassion to those characters who suffered from the verdict of the popular culture about outside beauty.

Grotesques are typically characterized by what they lack: fixity, stability, order. People or readers in particular can move a step further to add these modalities at play on the boundaries and nowhere else. To put it more bluntly, the grotesque is a boundary creature and does not exist except in relation to a boundary, convention, or expectation.

Boundedness is a critical feature of the grotesque's relationship with both the beautiful and the sublime Most people identify themselves being the oppressed, experience in one way or another, the societal conflict and the problem of dualities or binaries. In Quasimodo's part, the whole of Paris enjoys hearing the sounds of the bells but people despise the appearance of the bell ringer. He loves the bells and treats them as his best friends though their sounds make him deaf.In the scene with Esmeralda, it implies the complete opposite sides of the "spectrum of beauty". The most beautiful woman in Paris must look at the ugliest man in Paris, confronting the fact that beauty lies within.

The idea of equality attracts the readers to unravel and discover what lies behind the external sight. The idea of physiognomy or the belief that one's outside appearance dictated one's character traits is proven to be false under different circumstances presented in the narratives.

CONCLUSIONS AND RECOMMENDATIONS

The recognition of the grotesque as a phenomenon particularly relevant to modernism has been common to writers from Victor Hugo on, but with an increasing emphasis on the ambiguity and the dissolution of reality in the modern day. It is appropriate, then, that the act of definition should gain new ambiguity in the terms relevant to our own day, in the three fold division of media, mediator and mediation out of which the contemporary lens is constructed.

The Millennials' affection to scary stories can be traced even from the classic form of literature. The element of human nature's inclination to the oppressed or the victim, leads to the interest of the readers towards the character. The modern society demands for something unusual that depicts the realistic aspect. The new generation aims for something distinct that marks their strange inclination to scary stories.

In the local scene, it is the sad reality that the Philippine society is greatly under the spell of colonial mentality. Due to this fact, we place high priority on physical beauty and perfection. However, our perception of beauty is incredibly distorted. We see beauty and perfection through another culture's eyes---the colonizer's eyes. We do not perceive our own race to possess distinct beauty---what with the brown skin, short stature, thick lips, flat nose, and all the features that gives the Filipino an identity. We have been brainwashed by countless advertisements that "Black is dirty and white is beautiful" (though in most cultures the belief is entirely reversed). We have been convinced that being fair-skinned, hooked-nosed, wide-eyed, and long-haired is the standard that we must measure ourselves against. This notion is flawed. The grotesque truth: The Filipino has yet to feel completely comfortable in his or her own skin.

The influence of cultural and social variables on consumer behavior is a cornerstone of marketing. A cursory review of leading consumer behavior textbooks shows that most begin with an overview of the impact culture has on the behavior of the consumer. Perhaps no industry offers insight into the impact of the society on the individual than the cosmetics industry. Society dictates what is perceived to be attractive. The whims, desires and sense of fashion of the consumer require that the cosmetic industry continuously offer different and more advanced products. As society changes, so does the perception of beauty. (Hunt, et al, 2011)

It is therefore encouraged that the teachers, being the basic facilitator of learning situation, should have a wide understanding of their learners' needs in terms of the materials that will be utilized in the process. Although contemporary literary materials will be used, it is a must that they have enough knowledge of the traditional type for proper discussion and possible assimilation. The teachers may also encourage their students to read thematerials or use them as a spring board/major reading selection.

LITERATURE CITED

Connelly, F. (ed.) (2003). Modern Art and the Grotesque. Kansas City, KS: Cambridge University Press.

Fingesten, P. (1984). Delimitating the Concept of the Grotesque. The Journal of Aesthetics and Art History, 42(4), 419-426

Hapham, G. (1982). On the Grotesque: Strategies of Contradiction in Art and Literature. Princeton, N.J.: Princeton University Press.

Harpham, G. (1976). The Grotesque: First Principles. The Journal of Aesthetics and Art Criticism, 34(4), 461-468.

Hornedo F.H. (1999). Challenges to literacy education in the 21st century.UNITAS, 72 (4), 493-498.

Hunt, K. A. et al (2011). Cultural and Social Influences on the Perception of Beauty: A Case Analysis of the Cosmetics Industry. Journal of Business Case Studies, 7(1), 1-10.

Kayser, W. (1981). The Grotesque in Art and Literature, trans. Ulrich Weisstein. New York: Columbia University Press.

Makaryk, I. R. (ed.) (1993). Encyclopedia of Contemporary Literary Theory: Approaches, Scholars, Terms. Toronto, Canada: University of Toronto Press Incorporated.

Steig, M. (1970). Defining the Grotesque: An Attempt at Synthesis. The Journal of Aesthetics and Art Criticism, 29(2), 253-260.

Yates, W. (1997). An Introduction to the Grotesque: Theoretical and Theological Considerations. Cambridge: William B. Eerdmans Publishing Company.

Yates, W., & Adams, J. L. (ed.) (1997). The Grotesque in Art and Literature: Theological Reflections. Cambridge: William B. Eerdmans Publishing Company.

CHAPTER 4

Hispanic Poems in Philippine Literature: Materials in teaching Regional Culture and History

Published in The Normal Lights Volume 14, No. 1 (2020)

ISSN1646-4413

ABSTRACT

This paper discussed the use of Hispanic poems as sources of Filipino culture and local historical data (directly or indirectly mentioned in the poems), in teaching regional culture (of Bicol) and history. The poems are originally written in Spanish language and are translated into English by Hornedo. The analysis employed qualitative-descriptive approach of literary criticism, anchored on the theory of New Historicism and formalist- contextualist approach. In particular, the analysis delved on the content rather than on form and structure. Findings revealed that the poems are good sources of information about the image of the places in terms of physical and cultural milieu. Furthermore, the poems were found to be reflective of reliable materials in understanding Bicol soil and of the way of life of its inhabitants. These findings suggest that literature and history be taught side by side with original materials from a certain locality that eventually unveil cultural identity.

Keywords: *Formalism, new historicism, Philippine literature, regional culture and history*

INTRODUCTION

The primary aim of teaching literature is the appreciation and understanding of life through expressions of shared human experiences in various oral, written, and visual forms. Hence, it is highly imperative for a teacher of literature to employ appropriate approaches and use suitable materials to develop appreciation, and creative and critical responses in learners. According to Connors (2010), in order to justify one's readings, it is necessary to consider some clear and lucid theoretical account of what is admissible in reading. Literature requires breadth of dispassionate scholarly knowledge of other literature, of history, of psychology, and other related arts.

Teaching Regional Culture and History

It is important to note that Literature is not simply a product of History. It also actively makes history. The role of the author in any literary product is primarily determined by historical circumstances. In the article, Literature as a Historical Source (Toward the Historiography of the Problem), Mironets (1978) tackles the development of the history discipline. He stresses its demands with increasing imperiousness study of questions pertaining to its interaction with other fields and other modes. Accordingly, they include "perceiving historical reality, particularly the connections between historical scholarship and literature" (Mironets, 1978 p.57). Hence, new historicists see literature as actively involved in the making of history through its participation in discursive practices.

In the Philippine perspective, Hornedo (2000) discusses the 19th century Philippine literary relations as evident in the Antologia Poetica of Melendreras. The literary relations of Filipino writing can be traced through readings of such anthology. The Filipino literature written in the native languages of Hispanized cultural communities also serve as literary legacy. This study agrees to the idea of O'Brien

(1968), who posits the significance of regional studies in the development of a country. He emphasized:

It seems that no one can get a true and complete picture of Philippine history or what have been the formative influences on the nation's culture unless successful attempts have been made to gather and preserve historical, linguistic, and cultural data of various regions of the country and its people. (O'Brien, 1968, p.1)

Similarly, Hornedo (1997) advanced the role of regional identity in national development. "Regional identity therefore, becomes a matter of pride because it is the contribution of the region to the nation and not because it enables the region to surpass all the other regions." (Hornedo, 1997, p.58). Hence, both O'Brien and Hornedo believe that literary materials are important contributions to regional identity. The latter stresses that "region is constitutive of the nation and that the nation is a family of regions whose benefit is defined by the well-being and prosperity of its components." (Hornedo, 1997, p.58)

Materials for Teaching Culture and History

Hornedo (2000) states that literature can be taught considering the four reality frames, namely: literature as a theme; literature as script; literature as aesthetics; and literature as history. It finds ally in Lumbera and Lumbera's book (1997) which presents both history and anthology of Philippine literature". He also mentions in the same book the need for integration of research and evaluation, and translation of regional literatures in order to understand and appreciate one's regional identity.

There are about 70 Philippine languages, eight of which are considered major and possess extensive recorded literature. The number of the said literature excludes those written in English and Spanish. According to Lumbera (1997), with the exception of Tagalog, English, and Spanish literatures, the histories of various literatures remain in need of intensive research. He suggests that the literary scholar can also act as a historian in order to integrate the discussion of regional vernacular literature into an overall study of Philippine literature. He further suggests that translations may be deemed necessary to recognize the achievement of regional writers.

The Nature of New Historicism

The new historicism is defined as ''a mode of critical interpretation which privileges power relations as the most important context for texts of all kinds (Brannigan, 1998). It means treating the literary text as a space where power relations are obvious and easy to notice. The idea of 'power relations' refers to the connection of the text to the subject that sees literary participation in the course of history. It adheres to the practice of literary analysis to highlight the interrelatedness of all human activities. It also provides a more complete understanding of a text through its narrative discourse.

The Formalist-contextualist Approach

This type of formalism is a kind of literary criticism that deals with the content rather than the structure of the material under study. The main contention of this approach is to focus on the aesthetics to reveal the message of the text. Accordingly, formalism views literature as a special mode of language and proposes a fundamental opposition between poetic/literary language and the practical/ordinary language. Literary language is self-reflexive, which is referred to as 'literariness" of Jacobson (1969).

FRAMEWORK OF THE STUDY

This paper is anchored on the idea that the literary content of poems can be used in identifying historical facts. The aesthetics in the poems do not necessarily affect the message. Similarly, the text is connected to a subject with relevance to the course of events. The Formalist-contextualist approach and the New Historicism pave way in presenting cultural history as well as literary relations. Those are relevant to the idea of Hornedo (2000) that identifies the four reality frames in teaching literature, one of which is teaching literature as history where the sociological and cultural background of the six poems translated in English are considered to reveal the milieu embedded in the poems. Likewise, the theory of New Historicism as used in this paper defined as "reconstructs literary texts as historical objects by considering documents and methods previously excluded from traditional literary and aesthetic study" (Makaryk,1993, pp.124-128). Both regional and national identity can be deciphered from literary materials written during a particular time.

Objectives

This paper's major goal is to analyze some literary materials, Hispanic poems in particular, as part of regional literature. The main intention is to come up with authentic materials from the Bicol region and to highlight the identity of Bicol soil from the said poems to prove that the Hispanic poems can be good sources of understanding one's history and culture.

Specifically, this paper primarily aims to initially trace the themes of the English translation of the Hispanic poems. The context and content of the poems are also considered in understanding one's history. Second, to prove that the poems serve as both Hispanic legacy and regional literary materials as source of information on history. Then, to reveal both material and non-material culture in the early times during Spanish colonialization. Finally, to serve as a proof that Ibalong, the popular Bicol epic is indeed another Spanish poem and not an oral epic.

METHODOLOGY

Research Design

This paper employed descriptive design. It is a type of literary criticism intended to trace historical facts from the literary materials.

The content of the six poems were analyzed rather than their form. The implied period and setting when they were constructed form part of basis in their chronological presentation in this paper.

The Materials

The six poems under study are part of the archived collection of fifty-four poems of a Franciscan Priest, Father Bernardino Melendreras. They come in a typescript form with introduction by Father Pastrana-Riol. The English version of poems were published in the book of Dr. Hornedo, Culture and Community in the Philippine Fiesta and Other Celebration.

The Poet

Father Bernardino Melendreras, a native of Gijon, Spain arrived in Manila on February 11, 1893. In 1844, after his five years of stay in the Philippines, he served in Quipayo and Bombon in Camarines. He was then transferred to Libmanan after a year then back to Bombon in 1846. In the year that followed, he served in Libmanan for more than 20 years. In 1865, he was then assigned in the parish of Guinobatan, in Albay province, where he stayed with an anthropologist named Feodor Jagor. He died in Manila at the age of 52 in 1867. He had left a collection of 54 poems, called Antologia Poetica. They were written in a 32 x 22 cm paper with 98 leaves of poetry where text is only on one side. The six poems were translated into English by Dr. Florentino Hornedo.

The Translator

Dr. Florentino Hornedo is a literary icon whose interests include the field of anthropology, philosophy, literature, social science, ethnology, and history. He is a poet, painter, and sculptor aside from being a multi- awarded book author. His translations of Melendreras' poems, which are materials of this study, are his personal selections from among the collection of poems. He explained that Melendreras was one of the Spaniards from Peninsular Spain. He was a well-read poet and brought in literary trends of the time and was heavily influenced by current Iberian trends.

The Locale

Region 5, also known as Bicol region, is composed of six provinces, four of which—Camarines Norte, Camarines Sur, Albay, and Sorsogon—are geographically connected, while two of which—Masbate and Catanduanes—are island-provinces. The region has long been referred to as Ibalon as described by Scott (1994). The word ibalong was also the old name of Sorsogon Bay.

Study Context

Analysis of the poems delved more on context and content rather than form and elements of poetry. The themes of the poems unveil the material and non-material culture of the locale. Moreover, the identified custombrismo style supports the understanding of the background of the places where Melendreras stayed. For validation purposes, those places in the Bicol region were also traced and discussed.

FINDINGS

The analysis is divided into three parts: the description of the themes interpreted from the translated poems, the discussion of each poem based on their context and content that helped understand one's history, and the presentation of the deciphered material and non-material culture from the poems.

The sequence used in presenting the analyses of the six poems was based on the inferred ideas through historical details. Similarly, the material and nonmaterial culture of the region were identified based on the historical texts deciphered from each poem.

The Translated Hispanic Poems and their themes

Table 1 contains the titles of the translated poems and their deciphered themes. The poet's collection significantly identifies the nature of the Bicol soil and its ancient way of life. On this note, the contemporary teachers of Literature may discuss the poems with consideration of the themes and relevance to historical ideas.

Along with the themes of the poem, their tone is also important to consider in analyzing them. Tone indicates the mood or attitude of the poetic persona, thereby helping identify the message or the purpose of the poet.

Table 1.   The thematic aspect of the poems

The poems	The themes
1. The Mountain Dweller (El Igorote)	The idea of existence and survival in the society
2. *The Mountains of Bicol (Los Montes Del Bicol)*	The exotic but grandeur dwelling place
3. *To My Companions After Having Visited 3.The Cave of Colapnitan on 11 August 1861* *(A MisCompañeros, Despues De Haber Visitado La Cueva De* *Colapnitan El 11 Agosto De 1861)*	The gothic versus the awesome beauty of nature
4. *To a Friend (Un Amigo)*	Companionship and Solitude
5. *To The Rivulet Aslon (Al RiachueloAslon) Despedida*	On leaving and living
6. *To a Friend Who Asked Me for Verses* *(A Un Amigo Que Me Pidio Versos*	Customary threat and inspiration

The first poem discusses the life of early inhabitants of the place that can be philosophically regarded as the idea of existence and survival. The second poem reveals the importance of the prominent mountains in Bicol that serve as the dwelling place of animals that may now be considered as endangered. The ironic reality on the gothic side of a place as an awesome presentation of nature's beauty is the theme of the third poem. It encompasses the idea that not all gloomy and dark are morbid; they are also sources of exquisiteness and splendor. The binary idea of companionship and solitude is evident in the fourth poem, where the poet considers Mayon volcano as his only companion during his solitude, day and night. It implies that the place was sparsely populated and there was an obvious lack of technological advancement.

The fifth poem suggests the choice between leaving the place in order to live and affection to it as his reason to stay. The theme of the last poem unveils the decade-long amazement of the poet towards the way of life of the Bicolanos who withstand volcano's constant threat of eruption amid its majestic presence.

The context and content of the Poems in understanding one's history

Mountain Dweller

The poem Mountain Dweller describes the features and the kind of life of the native inhabitants of Bicol. Accordingly, the Spanish missionaries refer to the mountain-dwellers as Igorote until the 19th century. However, it may be the Dumagat rather than the Remontados who were originally referred to by Melendreras. The former are commonly called Negritos to whom the Agtas belonged based from the negritoethnolinguistic group. The first three lines of the poem state:

Jungle Man from Isarog am I,

A stranger to enslavement

I'm happy because I'm free,

It can be traced that Agta tribes are distributed in various regions of Luzon such as Regions 1, 2, 3, and 4, while some inhabit the mountainous areas of Camarines Norte and Camarines Sur. They are typically short, with dark skin and kinky hair, thick lips and have small noses. With the help of the National Commission on Indigenous People (NCIP), some are given the chance to attend school and be part of the mainstream community. In the early years, they simply adopt the name of the family whom they worked for and lived within the same household.

Also mentioned in the poem are the remontados which got its name from remontar, a Spanish verb which means "to flee to the hills", "to frighten away", and "go back to the mountains". The Remontados were believed to be descendants of those who lived in the plains but preferred to go up in the mountains during the early Spanish occupation to avoid conquest. Consequently, due to intermarriage between them and the negrito groups, also called Dumagats, they were later called tagabundok (mountain dweller) or magkakaingin (slash-and-burn farmer).

The mention of Mt. Isarog asserts itself as the second highest mountain in the region given the physical features which the poem highlights. The dramatic situation in the poem suggests that the inhabitants in the mountain mainly include wild animals such as boars, deers, monkeys, serpents, and other reptiles, which were considered as the source of nourishment or exotic type of food during that period.

The jungle is my palace
Conquerors of a thousand
Wild boars and deers
And of monkeys innumerable

The colossal serpents
I feed on their meats

I conquer wild beasts and reptiles
I'm the king of Isarog

The speaker in the poem, "I," seems to be very robust and uses ancient weapons, bow and arrow. In addition, the poem highlights the view of the ocean which still abounds with dolphins and whales. Similarly, the last two stanzas imply that the voice in the poem lives a very simple life with his partner. Their only worry is their freedom that they may have found somewhere in Mt. Isarog.

The Mountains of Bicol

The second poem, The Mountains of Bicol, originally Los Montes Del Bicol, absolutely refers primarily to Mt. Isarog and Mt. Mayon, being that they are the prominent mountains in the Bicol region. Mt. Isarog is found in Camarines Sur, while Mt. Mayon is in Albay. The entire poem speaks of serenity from the detailed description of sound produced by every creature which dwells in the mountains.

The voice in the poem suggests expression of nature's beauty, which Melendreras puts as beauty during the day and during the night. Note the following lines: "By day, that grandiose hymn, incomparable; by night, the monotonous and harsh sound". It denotes the idea that the place was characterized as ancient peaceful environment, where one can glean no trace of electricity. Notice in the following lines: The mountains of Bicol are the home of beautiful serpents that inspire terror; of bees that gather up honey eagerly; and merry insects which imitate their ardour flying and buzzling in wild abandon

The poetic persona is aware of the creatures, from insects, wild animals, to reptiles and amphibians, which form part of the rich natural resources contributing to the general wonder of the place. The persona attributes to all these to God almighty. The image that one may envision of the locale in the poem is a mountainous place with sparse populated.

To My Companions after Having Visited the Cave of Colapnitan on 11 August 1861

The third piece, To My Companions after having visited the Cave of Colapnitan on 11 August 1861 (A MisCompañeros, Despues De Haber Visitado La Cueva De Colapnitan El 11 Agosto De 1861) could have been written by Father Melendreras in 1861. The poem implies dedication to someone who visited the Colapnitan cave in Libmanan, Camarines Sur. It can be interpreted that the person referred to as companion in the poems is Fedor Jagor, who was an anthropologist who lived with the poet in Libmanan. In the book, Travels in the Philippines, ideas on relics that were found in the same cave were mentioned (Jagor, 1965). In the poem El Ibal, Eugenio (1996) mentioned the cave as hantik (weaver ants). El Ibal was popularly known before as Bicol's epic, but later literary scholars found out that it was just another poem in Antologia Poetica of Father Melendreras.

The entire poem reveals that the poet is inspired by the physical form of the cave. The presence of exotic birds contrasts the word gothic. The Bicol word colapnit literally means, bat, hence the name of the cave.

The tourism website of Libmanan describes the cave in modern times in the following lines:

Libmanan Caves National Park is a protected area of the Philippines located in Barangay Sigamot in the municipality of Libmanan, Camarines Sur in Bicol Region. It is centered on the massive 2,856 meter-long Colapnitan Cave, the tenth longest cave in the Philippines. The park itself covers a total area of 19.4 hectares across the hilly farmlands of Libmanan, known to host at least 18 more limestone caves of varying lengths, shapes and wonder. It was established in 1934 by virtue of Proclamation No. 654. The park is famous as the habitat of thousand of bats whose guano has been gathered from the cave for decades. It is also home to swift lets and some great long-armed spiders of the species Phrynus, known to be poisonous.(Retrieved   from http://dbpedia.org:8890/page/Libmanan_Caves_National_Park   . Accessed on February 18, 2014)

To a Friend

The majestic Mayon Volcano could be the friend referred to in the fourth poem, To a Friend (Un Amigo) by poetic persona. The following lines prove the reference Mayon volcano as the friend.

In deep solitude

I spend nights and days, and it is my happiness to watch the furious rotound eminence of Mayon exploding, tempestuous giant, whom now I call my friend.

The poem suggests friendship that transcends through time and place as implied in the aforementioned lines. The dramatic situation implies that the image of Mayon volcano is anywhere in sight when one lives in the southern part of Camarines Sur and in Albay.

The poet describes the eruption of Mayon with word, furious rotound eminence, which is an oxymoron that implies his acceptance of ironic reality that despite the danger, the volcano possesses such a captivating beauty.

In a symbolic in-depth interpretation, Mayon signifies the Bicolano's strength and resiliency to face and to rise from the ravages caused by Mother Nature. Every eruption also becomes an opportunity for people to befriend other people. It may also point out to the satirical idea of Bobis (1997) in her novel, Banana Heart Summer, where she mentions, "one eruption, one mansion". She purposely means that every eruption is equivalent to one mansion of politicians who directly receives the calamity aid of the national government or other nations.

To the Rivulet Aslon

To the Rivulet Aslon (Al Riachuelo Aslon Despedida) can be interpreted and analysed based on the poet's leaving Guinobatan in in the early months of 1867 because of illness. On October 7, 1867, he arrived in Manila to seek treatment but he died a day after. The poem has an obvious sad tone which reveals farewell note to speaker's present sanctuary. The idea on bidding goodbye are suggested in the following lines:

The rivulet received my parting gifts
And, turned into a nymph, fell on her knees,
And said, "Bring with you the sky to your native haven".

The term rivulet may mean the Bicol river as it is anciently called tico, a native term which means bent or curved. Moreover, the word Aslon also means Ibalon, the old name of the region. In a general interpretation, the poetic persona is evidently bidding goodbye to the Bicol region where he stayed for more than two decades.

To a Friend Who Asked Me for Verses

This short poem, To a Friend Who Asked Me for Verses (A Un Amigo Que Me Pidio Versos), expresses the feeling of concern and apprehension of the poetic persona towards the Bicolanos, who may have served as inspiration for the poem. It mainly focuses on the likelihood of a volcanic eruption, which, despite the volcano's majestic appearance, constantly poses a threat to the inhabitants. Melendreras may have written this poem during his early years in the region, when he was not yet accustomed to the parishioners' way of life. The said ideas are evident in the following lines:

Can you tell, perhaps , because it is serene, that it does not harbour the fury and bitter rue with which by habit it floods that field with incandescent brimstones and sand?

The third stanza strengthens the anxiety of the voice in the poem; it mentions Cagsawa church, now a tourist attraction in Daraga. It is referred to in the poem as the ruins of Daraga. Historical data say the church was built in 1587 in the small town of Cagsawa. It was burned by Dutch pirates in 1636 but was rebuilt in 1724 by Franciscan Friars under Father Francisco Blanco. During that period, Daraga was only a barrio of Cagsawa. On June 12, 1772, Cagsawa was named Salcedo then later renamed as Daraga. It had passed through series of names, such as Budiao, Cagsawa, and Locsin. The name Budiao was given by Franciscan missionaries, while it was through RA 993 in 1954 which declared it as municipality of Daraga. However, five years later, RA 2805 changed its name to Locsin. The name Daraga was restored in 1967 through RA 4994 and in 2012, Daraga held its first Cagsawa Festival.

The deciphered material and Non Material culture in the poems

The two interrelated aspects of human culture are the physical objects and the ideas associated with it. Material culture refers to the resources, spaces, and objects that people associate themselves with. They include the entire environment around the community. The said physical aspects help define the society's beliefs, behaviors, perceptions, and perspectives. On the other hand, non-material culture refers to the nonphysical aspect such as values, norms, morals, beliefs, language, organizations, and institutions.

Moreover, one of the four qualities in which the vernacular temper finds expression, as listed by Galdon (1979) from the essay of Venus Salangsang (1978) refers to the romantic nature of Philippine literature. Accordingly, it expresses itself in the tradition of sensibility, the tradition of romance and the pastoral tradition. He discusses pastoral tradition as:

The pastoral tradition persists today in the reaction to progress and industrialization and consists of a nostalgia for rural surroundings, rural beauty, rural life. It is the ancient call to go back to one's beginnings, to one's childhood self, which all men experience. (Galdon,1979 p.13)

DISCUSSION

The thematic element of the six poems showed the various custombrismo style which also indicates history. The six poems are also in similar presentation and construction with the believed, Bicol epic, "Ibalong," which was later proven to have been written by the same poet, Melendreras. It was titled El Ibal in his book, AntologiaPoetica. In 2013, Realubit, a retired UP Professor and a

Bicol scholar, renounced that Ibalong is not a Bicol Epic but a long narrative poem of Father Melendreras. The idea was first published in the article of Hornedo (1984) in the Journal of Philippine Studies.

The custombrismo style is also depicted as the general tone of the six poems. Likewise, from the deciphered themes, all the translated poems can be treated as personal accounts of the poet during his stay in the Bicol region. The poems of Melendreras are somewhat similar to Antonio Pigafetta's narrative in his First Voyage. He was a part of a crew of 265 to 280 men in five ships who joined the voyage of Magellan. As discussed by Mojares (2002), Pigafetta's narration of the Philippines is driven by more pragmatic concerns of the expedition—the markings of the navigation routes, description of ethnological features, survey of natural resources, and initiation of political and trade contacts.

Accordingly, Pigafetta's account remains inadequately studied as text since it particularly pertains to the "discovery" of the Philippine islands. His narrative is considered both a distinct literary creation and a key source in Philippine historiography just like the Hispanic poems as materials in this paper. The mode of representation is determined not only by the anticipations of the narrator, but the actual experiences in the voyage in Pigafetta's case. In Melendrera's case, the lived experiences and the personal accounts of the poet served as actual representation and expression of the Bicol soil.

The poems also served as both Hispanic legacy and material in teaching regional culture and history. They are part of Philippine writings under the Spanish colonialism. The content analysis revealed material and non-material culture of the Bicol region. However, the poems do not carry the rudiments of a secular literature which marks the basic influence of this era. It is far from the awit (song) and corrido (metrical romance), the two narrative poems that are sung and chanted and never simply read (Eugenio, 1988).

The poems of Father Melendreras are also far from Balagtas' poems that establish their significance to Philippine history (Lumbera, 1997). Instead, it uncovers the sad reality that the long-known Bicol epic Ibalong is in fact, just another poem of a Spanish Friar. Nevertheless, this paper posed the idea that literature, history and cultural identity are always interrelated. In addition, Hornedo (2000) explains, "Culture is the mode and pattern of the encounter of humans with their environment. Mode is determined by horizon of consciousness; pattern is the recurrent method of human action vis-à-vis elements of the elements of environment. The method is guided by the horizon of consciousness of historical agents" (p.14).

The poems by Father Melendreras indeed represent an authentic literary legacy to the Filipinos in general, and the Bicolanos in particular. The first poem, The Mountain Dweller, focuses on the early inhabitants of the place; the second poem, Mountains of Bicol, highlights Mt Isarog and Mayon volcano as habitat of exotic and endemic wild creatures; the third poem, To My Companions After Having Visited The Cave of Colapnitan on 11 August 1861, presents the beauty of nature in Colapnitan Cave, which until now is considered as one of the tourists attractions in Camarines Sur (accessed from http://www.philchm.ph/featured-cave/); the fourth poem, To a Friend Who Ask me for Verses, regards Mayon Volcano as the poet's inspiration and constant companion day and night; the fifth poem, To the Rivulet Aslon, reveals the old name of Albay province; and the sixth poem, To a Friend Who Asked me for Verses, is considered to be dedicated to the Bicolanos with reverence to their way of life along with the threat of the majestic Mayon Volcano.

The six poems therefore may be used as literary materials discussing regional history. This paper's contention finds ally in the idea of Lumbera (1997) who states that "A course in Philippine Literature cannot be a simple chronology of 'masterpieces' or a parade of fine writers; otherwise Filipino literary works, given their roots in contact with the culture of colonizers, might appear as nothing but an array of pallid reflections or indigenized importations" (p 4).

This paper also adheres to the idea of Rizal in his annotation of the work of Antonio De Morga, in 1609, Sucesos de las Islas Filipinas, as mentioned by Mojares (2002) in the article, "Rizal Reading

Pigafetta." Rizal saw the Spaniard's work as a convenient peg for tracing a counter-narrative of the Filipino past. He further inquired into connections among Philippine and Malay languages and the links that could be drawn from the study of customs and material culture in the Malay region and the wider Asian continent. In the same manner, in this paper, the poems of Melendreras contain ideas on both material and non- material culture of the Filipinos, Bicolanos in particular.

CONCLUSIONS AND RECOMMENDATIONS

The study traced the themes of the six poems originally written in Spanish. As published materials translated in English, they served as Hispanic legacy and proof of the 19th century Spanish and Filipino relations. The poems revealed both material and non-material culture of Bicolanos.

Based on the materials used in this paper, history and culture are inherent in literary materials, Hispanic poems in particular. Those materials can be used in teaching Philippine literature, particularly regional literature. This paper studied six poems of Melendreras being authentic literary materials from the Bicol region that can be considered good sources of understanding one's history and culture. The poems can be used in teaching Bicol history and culture since they reveal ideas about the Bicol region, in terms of historical, cultural, and physical aspects. This goes without saying that aside from the popular genres like prose, both fiction and non-fiction type, as well as prose narratives such as legends, myths, and folktales, poems may also be used in the study of culture and history. In addition, the poems are regarded as 19th century relations as Hispanic literary expressions.

Moreover, this paper suggests that culture and history are always embedded in literature. Every genre hints a contextual representation of a particular period or era which any nation has experienced. In the case of poetry, it is indeed an expression not only of emotions but also of wide array of subjects that may be as old or older than history.

Furthermore, the poems reveal current Spanish romanticism, local color, and custombrismo involved as well as Spanish contemporary formal conventions. The tradition of "custombrismo,"as Hornedo (2000) points out is the description of local customs and practices designed to awaken the public to the variety of cultural forms and institutions. Apparently, the same idea was applied by Rizal in his novels, such as allusions to myths and legends, types of food, children's games folksongs, and rituals.

For further study, this researcher recommends that other poems from various regions of the country be traced and be used in teaching local culture and history. Literary materials from respective places may provide rich source of people's way of life and ancient customary practices. Literary materials written in various respective regional languages may also be translated for wider dissemination and understanding of Filipinos and the entire global community toward cultural understanding and social identity.

REFERENCES

Bobis, M. (1997). Banana heart summer. Quezon City, Philippines: Anvil Publishing.

Brannigan, J. (1998). New historicism and cultural materialism. New York: St. Martin's Press.

Connors, C. (2010). Literary theory; A beginner's guide. United Kingdom: Oneworld Publications.

Eugenio, D. (1996). Philippine folk literature: The legends. Philippines: University of the Philippines.

Eugenio, D. (1988). Awit and corrido: Philippine metrical romances. Philippines: University of the Philippines.

Galdon, J. (1979) Essays on the Philippine novel in English. Manila, Philippines: Ateneo De Manila University Press.

Hornedo, F. (1984). Handiong: An original poem by Fr. Bernardino Melendreras, OFM. Philippine Studies, 32(4), 526–528.

Hornedo F. (1997). Pagmamahal and pagmumura. Quezon City, Philippines: Ateneo De Manila University Press.

Hornedo, F. (2000). Culture and community in the Philippine fiesta and other celebrations. Manila, Philippines: UST Publishing House.

Jacobson, R. (1969). Language in literature. Massachusetts, MS: Harvard University Press.

Jagor, F. (1965). Travels in the Philippines. Philippines: The Filipiniana Book Guild.

Lumbera, B., & Lumbera, C. (1997). Philippine Literature revised edition, A history & anthology. Quezon City, Philippines: Anvil Publishing Inc.

Lumbera, B. (1997). Revaluation: Essays on Philippine literature, cinema & popular culture. Manila, Philippines: UST Publishing House.

Makaryk, I.R. (ed) (1993). Theory on New Historicism in The encyclopedia of contemporary literary theory, approaches, scholars, terms (pp.124-128). Canada: University of Toronto Press.

Mironets, N.I. (1978). Literature as a historical source (Toward the historiography of the problem). Soviet Studies in History, 17(2), 57-84.

Mojares, R. (2002). Waiting for Mariang Makiling. Essays in Philippine cultural history. Philippines: Ateneo de Manila University Press.

O' Brien, J. (1968). The Historical and cultural heritage of the Bikol people. Naga City, Philippines: Ateneo De Naga Press.

Realubit, M.L. (2013, September 13). Bicolmail. Retrieved from http://www.bicolmail.com.

Scott, W.H. (1994). Barangay sixteenth–century Philippine culture and society. Ateneo De Manila University Press.

Salangsang, V. (1978). Directions for Philippine literary criticism. Budhi Papers Essays in Literature 1, pp. 20-2. Quezon City, Philippines: Ateneo De Manila.

CHAPTER 5

Water On Bicol West Coast: Material and Non-Material Culture

Co-author – Rey Dennis L. Gilbas.

Published in Ecology. Environment. & Conservation. 26 (2): 2020

EM International ISSN 0971–765X

ABSTRACT

Water is always treated traditionally in its environmental context. It is always regarded as part of the natural sciences and studied in terms of ecological aspects including physical and geographic. In this paper, water is considered as both material and non-material culture of the community. It focused on the anthropological approach that deals with water utilization, valuation and perspectives on water safety of the residents in the municipality of Bulan, Sorsogon. The study used qualitative data gathering through field and direct observations and focus group discussions. Thematic analysis was employed from the informants' in-depth interviews. This paper found out that the socio-economic aspect of the community was affected by the availability of water, water use, and how people value water. The population growth, communal activities and climate change affected local residents' perspective on water. Hence, water is a material and non-material culture of the community which require a continuous process of adaptation. It is recommended that each resident and various agencies in the local community should have cumulative effort to sustain safe and practical use of water, an indispensable societal culture.

Keywords: *Water, Bicol west coast, Material and Non-material Culture, Bulan, Sorsogon*

INTRODUCTION

Water and Culture are inseparable elements of hu- man life". It was stated by the United Nations Educational, Scientific, and Cultural Organization (UNESCO) as key water and culture messages on the occasion of World Water Day 2006. Accordingly, culture should be regarded as the permanently evolving set of distinctive spiritual, material, intellectual and emotional features of society or a social group. To quote the article of the World Health Organization (WHO), the following are other ideas on water in relation with culture:

1. It encompasses – in addition to art and literature – lifestyles, ways of living together, value systems, traditions and beliefs. The way water is used and valued constitutes an integral part of a society's cultural identity. 2. Foster the dialogue of cultures to find solutions for water-related problems. Cultural diversity, stakeholder involvement and intercultural dialogue should be the guiding principles for the development of awareness raising, educational and capacity building material and methods. 3. Pro- mote inclusive, solution-oriented water governance that takes into account all facets of cultural diversity and that seeks informed consensus. Indigenous knowledge holders should be involved as full partners. 4. Encourage the artistic expression on water issues as an important means of fostering under- standing and sharing information. Drawings, photographs, audiovisual materials and the performing arts often help to get messages across cultural and language borders. 5. Encourage the creation, transition and dissemination of information on water and

culture in your community. Involve schools, universities, those in your work-place and at home. (WHO, 2006)

Given the abovementioned discussion on water as an important cultural factor, the World Health Organization is indeed encouraging the study and the dissemination of information on the cultural aspect of water. The WHO works on aspects of water, sanitation and hygiene (WASH) where the health burden is high and where evidence-based interventions could make a major difference. As a direct action to the call, this paper poses a collaborative work of representatives from government institutions, the Bulan Water District (BWD) as the water agency and the Sorsogon State College (SSC) as an aca- deme. Both are responsible to maintain and foster information through literacy campaign on the issue of safe and sustainable water supply in the community.

The BWD supplies the water requirement of the municipality of Bulan which is situated in the West Coast of Bicol. It was formed in 1975 and acquired the ownership and management of the entire system in accordance with Presidential Decree No. 198, otherwise known as the Provincial Water Utilities Act of 1973. At present, with the onset of the climate change, BWD is experiencing problems maintaining an adequate level of service in keeping up with the progress and the population demand of the municipality. Aside from the technical problems such as inadequate water supply especially during dry sea- son, absence of interconnections in some parts of the distribution system, the illegal connections which lead to leakages is one of the common problem. It can be attributed to the concessionaires' attitude and way of life without regard to water safety.

On the other hand, Sorsogon State College (SSC) is formerly called the Sorsogon College of Arts and Trades (SCAT). It was established in 1907 and after 86 years, was converted into a state college in 1993 by virtue of Republic Act. It is composed of four campuses namely Sorsogon City Campus, Bulan Campus, Magallanes Campus and Castilla Campus. It has four mandates which include instruction, research, extension and production. This paper in- tends to form part mainly of the research and extension services of the academe through cultural study of water in the municipality of Bulan. Furthermore, it also adheres to provide literacy program on water safety in terms of cultural practices of consumers.

Material And Nonmaterial Culture

The two interrelated aspects of human culture are the physical objects and the ideas associated with it. The material culture refers to the resources, spaces and objects that people associate themselves with. To mention some, they include offices, schools, churches and the entire environment around the community. The said physical aspects help define the society's beliefs, behaviours, perceptions and perspectives. On the other hand, nonmaterial culture refers to the nonphysical aspect such as values, norms, morals, beliefs, language, organizations and institutions.

In this paper, the water is treated as both material and nonmaterial aspect of culture of the residents of Bulan, Sorsogon. It is material being an indispens- able resource of the community and at the same time, nonmaterial in terms of how people value its use and considered as an important factor in their way of life.

Water System in the Philippines

The Asian Development Bank (ADB) presented a study on Water Supply and Sanitation Sector, As- sessment, Strategy and Road Map in the Philippines in 2013. Accordingly, in the Philippines, water sys- tems are classified into one of three levels: Level I, stand-alone water points (hand pumps, shallow wells, rainwater collectors); Level II, piped water with a communal water point (bore wells, spring systems); and Level III, piped water supply with a private water point (a household service connec- tion). The World Health Organization (WHO)– United Nations Children's Fund (UNICEF) Joint Monitoring Programme (JMP) reported in March 2012 (the JMP March 2012 Report) that the Millen- nium Development Goal (MDG) of 92% coverage has been met for drinking water.

The Locale of the Study and its Brief History

In 2001, Bulan celebrates her 200th year anniversary or bicentennial, since it was refounded along the banks of the Mariboc River. Its history can be traced back prior to the Spanish period. Stated below is the excerpt of historical accounts of Bulan: Archeological evidences point out that long be- fore the coming of the Spaniards, the coasts of Sorsogon were already thriving with communities and settlers dating back to as early as 4,000 B.C., when the Indonesians reached Southern Luzon. The archeological findings excavated in san Juan, Magsaysay and Gate, which were evaluated to be- long to the Ming and Sung dynasty support the theories of historical researchers that the southern- most tip of Luzon, mentioned by Beyer and other Historians, probably including Bulan, sowed signs of civilization as far as 960 A.D. Golden Crowns, believed o exist from 91 B.C. to 79 A.D., were also excavated in Bulan.

Historical records disclose that in 1569, an expedition led by Captain Luis Enriquez de Guzman and Fray Alonzo Jimenez, an Augustinian Friar, reached Sorsogon soil and found a small settlement of natives engaged in fishing and farming. This settlement was believed to be Otavi. It was in Otavi where Fr. Jimenez, together with Fr. Juan Orta, celebrated the first mass in Luzon. On May 16, 1572, Capitan-General Miguel Lopez de Legazpi divided what is now Sorsogon Province into various encomiendas, and he allocated "Bililan"(Bulan) as a royal encomienda (Gilana, 1998).

The Historic Cultural Traits of the Filipinos in the Water Use

De Morga (2011) described the inhabitants of the Philippines with the following words, "The young and the old ordinarily bathe their entire bodies in the rivers and streams without regard to whether this may be injurious to their health, because they find it to be one of the best remedies to be healthy." He was referring to the Filipino's (then called Indio) habit of taking a bath every day. He noticed that the Filipinos dipped themselves into the river before sundown and then took a shower at his home using a tabo (dipper) to scoop water stored in earthenware jars and then shampooed hair using gugo (from the bark of Entada phaseikaudes). He called the said practice as "injurious to their health" because the Spaniards, just like other Europeans of that time, did not take a bath every day. The number of times people take a bath is culture- based. It depends on the type of climate in the area and the availability of water.

De Morga, (2011) also wrote his observation that Filipinos drink water as the Spanish would drink wine every dinner. He described that the Indios would eat rice together with a type of a certain dish and then pause to drink water and continue to eat and pause again to drink water. In contrast, he said that the Spanish would only drink water once he was finished with his meal. This manifests a cultural difference in terms of drinking water. Since water was very much available to Filipinos in earlier times, it was considered the number one type of drink that Fiipinos prefer. It is in comparison with the Americans who prefer milk and Chinese prefer tea. Until at present with the advent of modernism, even when Filipinos drink wine, juice, or soda together while dining, a glass of water still completes the meal.

It was further discussed by Castro (2015) in his article on Philippine Panorama that in Philippines, with humid environment one needs to take a bath every day, unlike in cold, arid regions where one's skin easily dries up because of frequent bathing. Once Filipinos migrate to temperate and polar countries, however, they still bring with them the practice of taking a bath every day as they feel un- clean (even if they don't sweat a lot) without doing so.

The aforementioned statements provide impact on the importance of water and the Filipinos cultural usage of water. The basic use of water was observed in the early times. In the more recent times, water use is innumerable and with more complication with the invention of the new technologies and facilities.

Other Studies on Water

According to ADB (2013), water districts, on the other hand, are not obligated by LWUA to plan or implement sanitation and sewerage projects, despite the mandate they have under Presidential Decree

198. It was however, pointed out that water districts which initiated sewerage projects increased their water tariffs, causing water bills to rise by 8%–50%. Lack of enforcement of existing laws and regulations is also a critical gap in the sector. Similar to water supply, the government's efforts in addressing the inadequacy of sanitation infrastructure are also constrained by a weak and fragmented regulatory framework, and inadequate monitoring mechanisms and financial resources. There are many institutions with sanitation-related mandates, but the responsibilities under these mandates are unclear. The leadership, which required to push efficient, effective, and sustainable sanitation programs, is also lacking. While the DOH plays a key role in the sector due to the health impacts of poor sanitation, the only unit at the DOH addressing sanitation is- sues is the Environmental and Occupational Health Office of the National Disease Control and Prevention Center, the mandate of which in sanitation is limited to policy formulation and monitoring.

In the study of Israel (2009) on Local Service De- livery of Potable Water in the Philippines: National Review and Case Analysis, he asserts that the poor quality of water from some water districts was due to water turbidity. It was due to natural and man- made factors as one of the key issues faced by the water districts. In addition, he identified denuded watersheds and water pollution that endanger both surface and underground water sources as one of the key issues affecting water service delivery as a whole. Furthermore, the following are also considered as issues affecting water key issues facing the LGU's which include lack of emphasis on sanitation as an important public function related to local water service delivery; weak and fragmented organizational structures resulting in inefficient local water service delivery; gender and age-insensitive planning and implementation of local potable water ser- vice delivery projects.

Based from the above cited studies, the research- ers aim to present the traditional and modern practices of the water concessionaires. It traces the needed plan of action necessary to answer the need for the sustainability of safe and potable water sup- ply. It also aims to instil awareness to the different agencies responsible to water maintenance, delivery and use.

Framework of the Study

This paper is anchored on the idea that communication and information are vital factors in the development of a society. The UNICEF (1999) called it as Communication for Development. It requires re- search and planned process for social transformation. Accordingly, it operates through three main strategies; advocacy to raise resources and political and social leadership commitment for development goals; social mobilization to build partnerships and alliances with civil society organizations and the private sector; and program communication for changes in knowledge, attitude and practice of participants.

Alongside communication for development, the idea on how water be treated as an object of anthropological inquiry intends to reorient and discipline the general public in connection with their practical uses, habits, custom and lifestyles. The study of Fielding (1992) on Determinants of household water conservation: The role of demographic, infrastructure, behavior, and psychosocial variables identifies that one way of promoting water conservation behaviors may be through developing a culture of water conservation in the household. Consequently, school- based education aids the process as it facilitates two-way influence processes between parents and children.

The current study adheres to the theory that there is a link between the communal culture on the utilization of water for a safer and healthier life and the societal responsibility on the knowledge and aware- ness of the individual member of each Filipino family. The household water use is a collective outcome and consistent to the psychosocial and cultural aspects.

Objectives

This paper aims to identify how the residents of Bulan, Sorsogon regard water as an important factor in the development of their community as a mate- rial and non-material culture. Specifically, it sought to identify the key issues related to water such as the water source, practices of the community along water utilization, valuing and safety. It also intends to propose actions to be administered to increase the stability of water as a form of academic extension program to the community.

METHODOLOGY

This paper used anthropological approach. It uti- lized the qualitative data gathering through field and direct observations and focus group discus- sions. Thematic analysis was employed from the informants' in-depth interviews. The guide ques- tionnaire was prepared in the mother tongue of the informants for easy comprehension. There are a to- tal of 110 key informants from the different zonal areas of Bulan, Sorsogon.

RESULTS AND DISCUSSION

Water Source of the Residents

There are various sources where the residents of Bulan, Sorsogon got their water supply. They were grouped into five. The table below shows such sources.

Majority of the residents got their water from water district. They are composed of 62.73% or 69

Table 1. Sources of Water of the Residents Bulan Water
District
Deep Well (electric pump)
Shallow well
Water refilling stations
Illegal connection from their neighbour

Sources of Water of the Residents

out of 110 informants. There are only 3 informants or 2.7% who got their water from their neighbours' faucets.

The interviews also revealed the comparison of water usage between those who have water installations and those who got water supply from other sources. Most of the concessionaires consume at least 250 gallons of water per month which costs them the minimum fee of P130.00. As compared to those who got from other sources, water district as water provider is deemed practical, economical and safe, considering the less health hazard and less expenses to the part of the consumers. Those who have water pumps may incur additional electric consumption without the assurance of safe under- ground water.

Similarly, those who got from shallow well need to exert extra effort in manual operation of the pump and in transporting the water from the well for household use. The water generated from both electric and manual pumps may not be sufficient to the needs of the consumers and it also poses threat to health as water may be contaminated different contaminants mainly from the septic tanks of the residents.

Water Utilization, Valuing and Safety

The informants are well aware of the importance of water. They were asked how do they value water and why they should use water practically and con servatively. They were also asked if they believe that water can be created and if they consider water as part of their life. The table below provides the matrix presentation of the saturated responses of the participants.

There are four saturated responses when they were asked on the practical and valuable use of water they are; mawawalan agad ng suplay ang iba (others will not have enough supply of water); importante an tubi sa pagbuhay (water is important in our everyday lives); namahalon ang bayadan (water bill increases); di na mapapalitan an tubi pag nawara (water cannot be replaced) The cited responses only adhere to the awareness and concern of the community towards the value of water and its use. How- ever, not one of the 110 informants have mentioned about health and safety regarding water and its source and availability.

When asked if they believe that water can be created, the old mythical idea surfaced that water can be simply dug out of the ground. Some informants answered, Mahukay na sana para makaalog, which can be literally translated to, "dig the ground to fetch water". Others mentioned that, yaa man an Bulan water district, which implies their trust to the water district to provide them water at all times. The said responses revealed the communal belief that water is always available and crisis is far at sight.

Nonetheless, the residents of Bulan also believe that water is a part of their culture. As such, they also consider that water is needed in order to enjoy life. Ordinary activities cannot be performed with- out water. When they were asked if they need to do something to lessen their water consumption and help in water conservation, positive responses were solicited. The top responses include, dire nakadanon sa komunidad pag nagsasayang nin tubi or it does not help in the community if water is wasted and dapat bawasan kan consumidores an pag gamit nin tubi asin gamiton sa tama, or the consumers should lessen their utilization of water and use it appropriately.

Table 2. Participants' top responses on water utilization, valuing and safety Water

Utilization and valuing	Water safety
Mawawalan agad ng suplay ang iba (others will not have enough supply of water)	*1. mayad na sana an nagpapakalakaga nin tubi* (it is better to boil water)
Importante an tubi sa pagbuhay (water is our everyday lives)	2. Mapatakod na sana kami nin tubi makabarato pa, kaysa
Namahaion ang bayadan (water bill increases)	magbayad sa ospital nin mahal (we will rather have water connection installed rather than paying hospital bills) important in
di na mapapalitan an tubi pag nawara (water cannot be replaced)	
	3. boiling water may also cost them more than paying water bills
	4. Just get water from the refilling station even if it will incur additional expenses

There are also suggestions from the informants as to how they can help in the water preservation. They are the following: Magtipid sa paggamit (Con- serve water use); magtanom san puno (plant trees); magtipon san tubi (provide stock water); and a remark- able comment from a few which says inspeksyonon an mga tubo/ o mga tagas (inspect possible water leaks). On the other hand, there is a saddening re- mark from ten or 9% of the total informants to just leave the issue to the Bulan Water District as they say, trabaho na sin Bulan Water District yuon.

There are also some cases of water-related sick- ness such as cholera and amoeba problems. From the responses, there are 17.27% or nineteen informants who positively confirmed that they had experiences of suffering from some illnesses related with water in the previous years. Out of further inquiry, it was revealed that most of those who suffered from sickness got their water from both deep and shallow wells. When asked on what they have real- ized out of the said experience, their responses led to the impact associated to their socio-economic status. One informant said, mayad na sana an nagpapakalakaga nin tubi (it is better to boil water); while others say, mapatakod na sana kami nin tubi makabarato pa, kaysa magbayad sa ospital nin mahal (we will rather have water connection installed rather than paying hospital bills). Some believe that boiling water may also cost them more than paying water bills while a few consider just getting water from the refilling station even if it will incur additional expenses.

According to the study, The State of Water Re- sources in the Philippines, published in June 2007 by Greenpeace Southeast Asia, the inefficiency in water usage was aggravated by the absence of regulations, economic incentives, and institutional arrangements needed to promote water conservation and rational use of water. Greenpeace is an independent global campaigning organisation that acts to change attitudes and behaviour, to protect and conserve the environment and to promote peace. The said idea holds true in the present study where the residents of Bulan Sorsogon are less concerned with their water utilization and safety. Although 43.63% or 48 of the informants believe that they should be re- sponsible in the water safety, the remaining percent- age considers Bulan Water District, Local Government unit and the Municipal Health Office as those in-charge in terms of safe water servicing.

CONCLUSIONS

The water concern can be associated with corporate social responsibility which adheres to the common good of every human being. Farsetta (2009) in his article, Water, the Newest Wave of Corporate Social Responsibility emphasized that both government and companies are responsible for ensuring clean drinking water which she indicated as " sustainability on world fresh and safe water". It only implies that every person should emanate ac- tion to help potable water sustenance through glo- bal awareness on water utilization which can be done through the conduct of further study and in- formation campaign.

Water is everybody's business and an indispens- able cultural entity of the community. Therefore, the action should emanate from each and every water concessionaire. The awareness and attitude of every individual matters. It is also recommended to adapt through local ordinances the full enforcement of the implementation of national laws concerning water use, protection and safety. The collaboration on the side of various government agencies, private enti- ties and civic organizations coupled with appropri- ate actions are also encouraged, since water crisis can not be solved overnight.

It is also a necessity that every public official, aca- demicians and businessmen, if not all individuals be equipped theoretically and technically on water uti- lization. It can be made possible through local, na- tional and foreign funded training programs to pro- vide total awareness and understanding on the im- portance of water to socio-economic stability, health, security and better living condition.

REFERENCES

Article Retrieved from http://www.who.int/ water_sanitation_ health/Water&culture Englishv2.pdf accessed on February 12: 2017.

Castro, N. 2015. Culture Current: The cultural relevance of water in the Philippines. Philippine Panorama retrieved from https://www.academia.edu/ 14486700/Culture_Current_The_cultural_ relevance_of_water_ in_the_Philippines

De Morga, A. 2011. Events in the Philippine Islands. National Historical Commission of the Philippines retrieved from http://nhcp.gov.ph/?s=events + in + the

+ philippine + islands

Gilana, A. 1998 A Brief History of the Town of Bulan retrieved from https://www.scribd.com/document/ 43812614/ A-Brief-History-of-the-Town-of-Bulan.

Greenpeace Southeast Asia, The State of Water Resources in the Philippines retrieved from http://www. greenpeace.org/seasia/ph/Global/seasia/report/ 2007/10/the-state-of-water-in-the-phil.pdf on March 12, 2017.

Israel, D. 2009. Local Service Delivery of Potable Water in the Philippines: National Review and Case Analysis. Phil- ippine Institute for Development Studies retrieved from http://dirp3.pids.gov.ph/ris/dps/pidsdps 0938.pdf

UNESCO Universal Declaration on Cultural Diversity, UNESCO, Paris 2002; see also http://portal.unesco. org/culture/en/ev.php-URL_ID=2450& URL_DO=DO_ TOPIC&URL_S ECTION=201.html